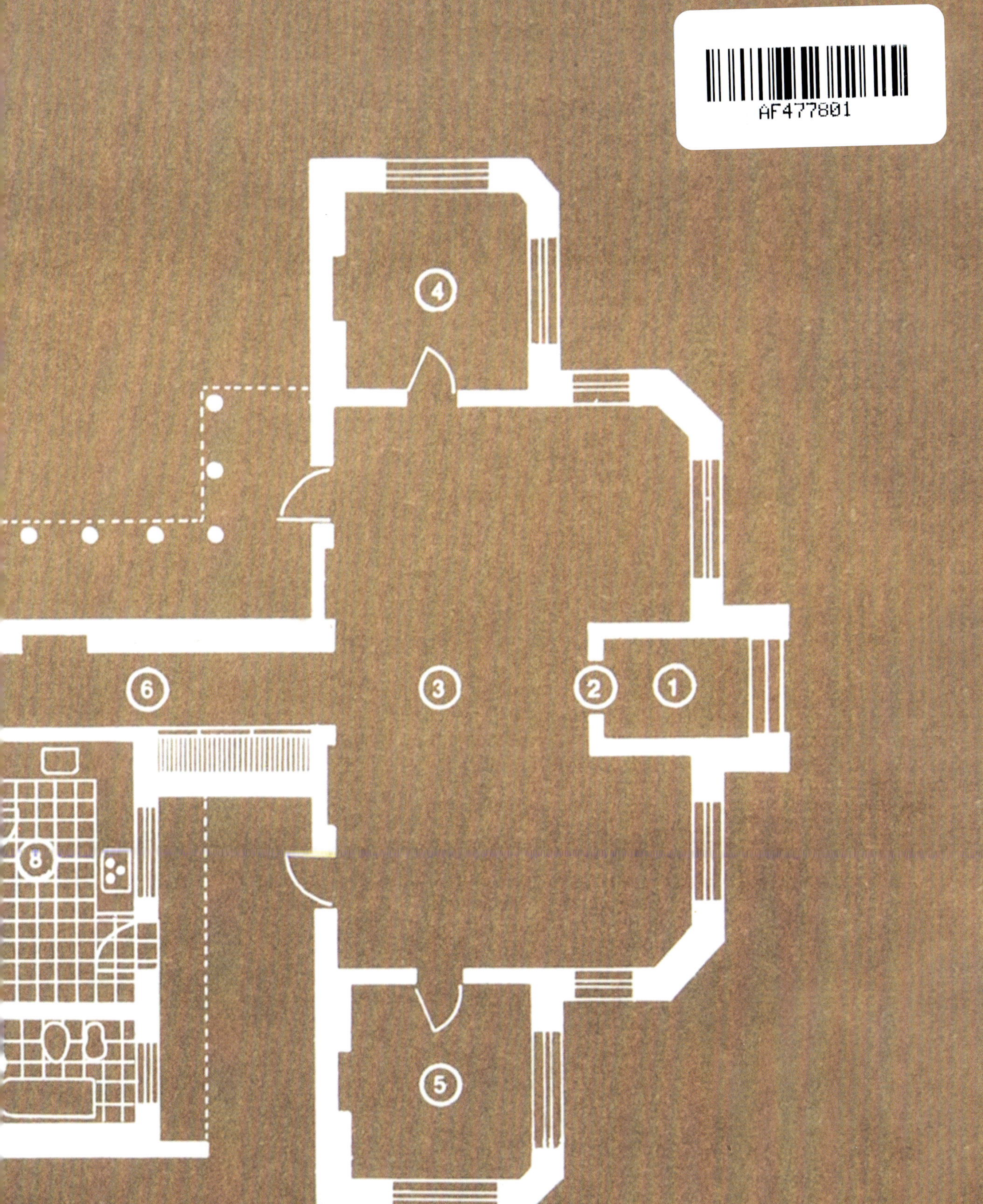
4
6
3
2
1
8
5

# CASA TOMADA

# SITELINES 2018
## —
# CASA TOMADA

## CURATORIAL TEAM

José Luis Blondet
Candice Hopkins
Ruba Katrib

## SITELINES 2018 TEAM

Brandee Caoba
John Cross
Irene Hofmann
Joanne Lefrak
Sage Sommer

## CURATORIAL ADVISOR

Naomi Beckwith

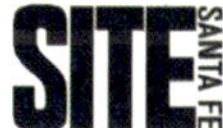

This catalogue accompanies the exhibition

# CASA TOMADA

*SITElines.2018: New Perspectives on Art of the Americas*
SITE Santa Fe, August 3, 2018 – January 6, 2019

Significant support provided by

**The Andy Warhol Foundation for the Visual Arts**

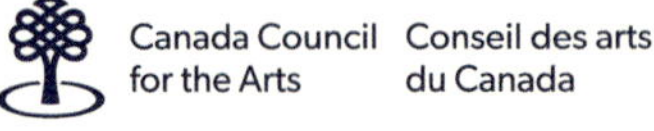


Endpapers are reproductions of the cover and an excerpted page from Juan Fresán's graphic translation of Julio Cortázar's "Casa tomada," published as *Casa Tomada* (Buenos Aires, ARG: Minotauro, 1969). Photographs Kyra Kennedy

# ARTISTS

Lutz Bacher | USA

Ángela Bonadies and Juan José Olavarría | VEN

Melissa Cody | USA

Paz Errázuriz | CHL

Victor Estrada | USA

Radamés "Juni" Figueroa | PRI

Andrea Fraser | USA

Hock E Aye Vi Edgar Heap of Birds | USA

Fernanda Laguna | ARG

Victoria Mamnguqsualuk | CAN

Jumana Manna | USA

Eduardo Navarro | ARG

NuMu (Stefan Benchoam and Jessica Kairé) | GTM

Tania Pérez Córdova | MEX

Jamasee Pitseolak | CAN

Naufus Ramírez-Figueroa | GTM

Eric-Paul Riege | USA

Curtis Talwst Santiago | CAN

Sable Elyse Smith | USA

Stephanie Taylor | USA

Lawrence Paul Yuxweluptun | CAN

# CONTENTS

Curtis Talwst Santiago, *Le Spam*, 2016, from *Infinity Series*, 2008–ongoing

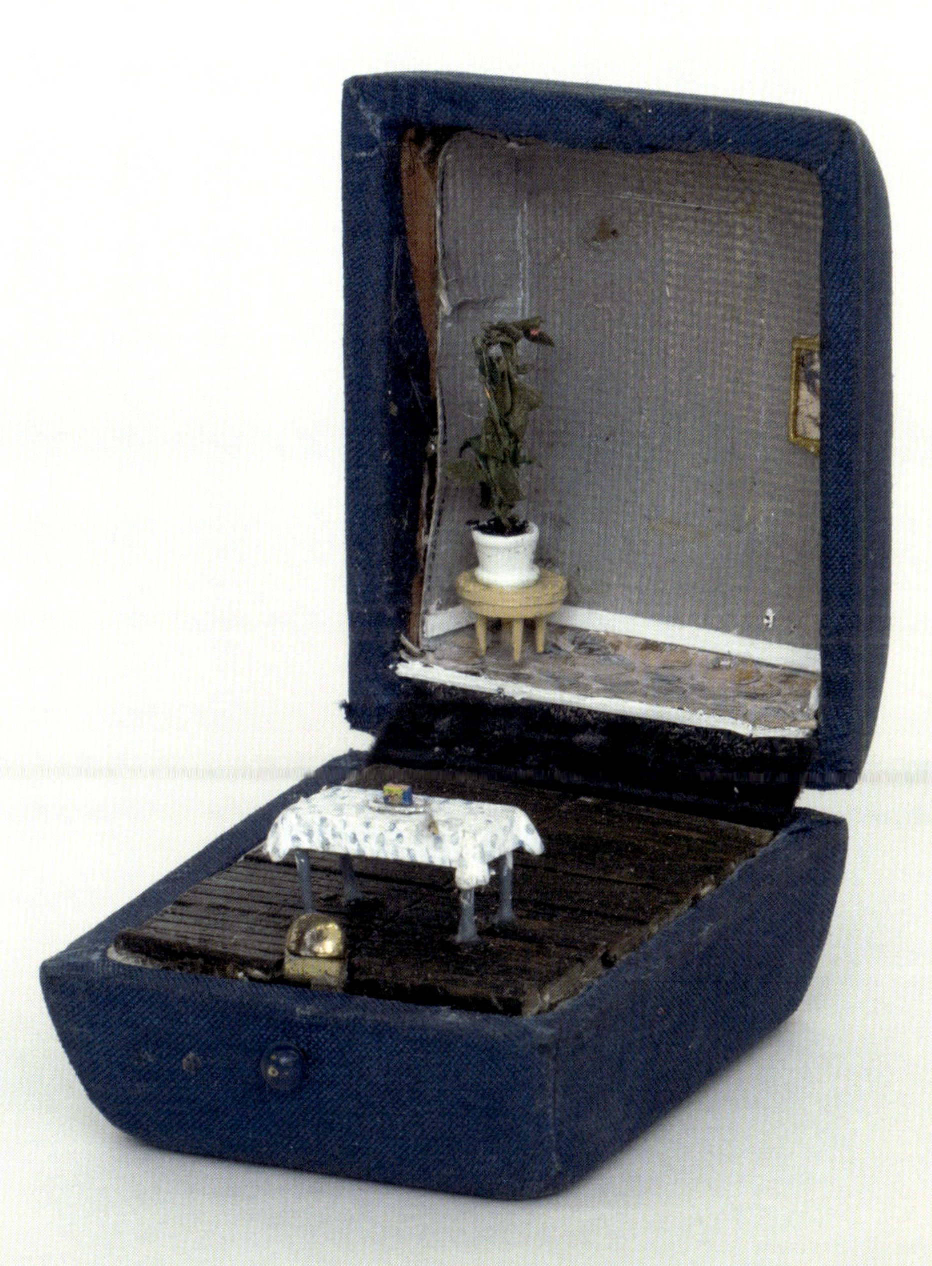

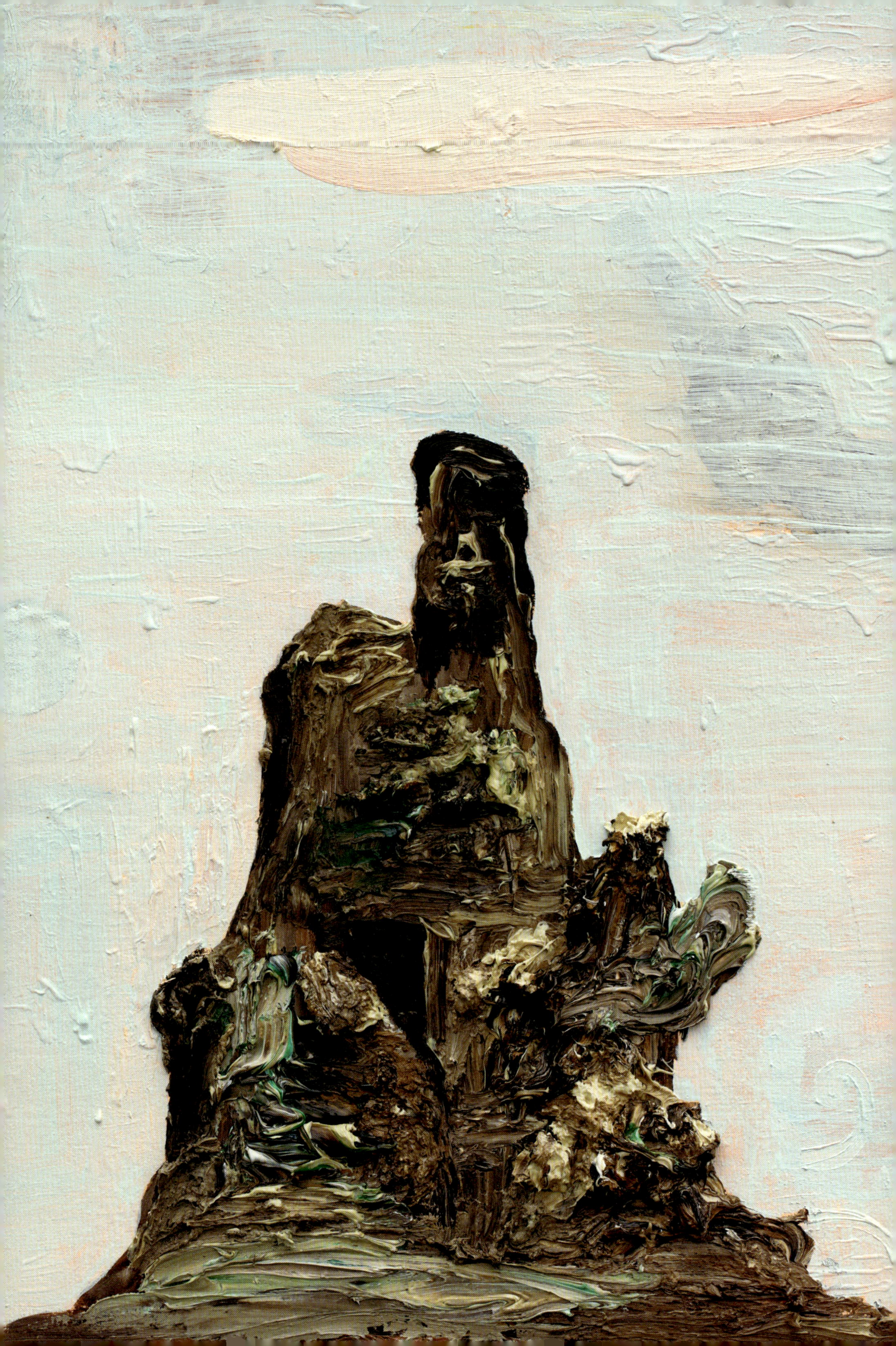

# FOREWORD

The biennial at SITE Santa Fe has been transformed over the last six years. A leader on the biennial scene for over twenty years, SITE opened in 1995 to present what was then the only international contemporary art biennial in the United States. Over the years, while the number of biennial exhibitions being presented worldwide grew exponentially, the format of the presentations, the lists of curators invited to organize them, and the rosters of participating artists remained remarkably narrow. Recognizing these leanings in the international biennial model, in the fall of 2010 we began exploring a new approach for our signature show. In the process of revisiting our history, we questioned all previous assumptions and expectations, and ultimately shifted direction.

What emerged was a new biennial series that, while reaffirming SITE's place in the vanguard of international contemporary art, provides the basis for a greater and more meaningful connection to place and community. With the 2014 launch of the biennial program, renamed *SITElines: New Perspectives on Art of the Americas,* we introduced a new set of principles to guide our work. We established a collaborative and multivocal approach to curating and tapped the potential for continuity between biennial exhibitions by building an infrastructure for long-term engagements with artists with whom we could realize community-based projects.

The most demonstrable and visible change to the program is the geographic focus of *SITElines: New Perspectives on Art of the Americas.* SITE's biennial now looks to place as a structural framework, to the history of New Mexico as an inspiration, and to the Americas as a vast territory for exploration. *SITElines* directs attention to the layers of history and culture embedded in Santa Fe and its surroundings, a rich microcosm of the Americas: before statehood, New Mexico was first a Native American land, and then, successively, a Spanish kingdom, a Mexican province, and a US territory. With *SITElines,* we link this fertile area to the rest of the Western Hemisphere, shifting from an east–west axis to one that runs south–north. Rejecting the notion of homogeneity in the Americas, we recuperate multiple histories and cosmologies, looking to artists to help us reveal and understand points of view that have often been sidelined in the contemporary art world.

*Unsettled Landscapes,* our first *SITElines* exhibition, was curated by a team of four, including two guest curators, Lucía Sanromán and Candice Hopkins, and two SITE Santa Fe curators,

Victor Estrada, *Pink Cloud / Chocolate Mountain / Blue Sky with Shadow,* 2017

Irene Hofmann and Janet Dees. A council of five curatorial advisors, whose fields of expertise covered Canada, the Caribbean, Central America, and South America, joined us in dialogue preparatory to the show. For the first time, SITE's biennial was organized collaboratively within a structure that invited multiple and varying voices into our curatorial discussions. With the vast potential of the Americas as a source of inspiration and provocation, the team decided to begin *SITElines* with an investigation of the land—a topic elemental, universal, and intensely present to those of us living in the American Southwest.

Two years later, we welcomed a team of five curators for the organization of *SITElines.2016*, including Rocío Aranda-Alvarado, Kathleen Ash-Milby, Pip Day, Pablo León de la Barra, and Kiki Mazzucchelli. Together they created a show featuring the work of thirty-five artists from sixteen countries, including eleven new commissions. This exhibition, titled *much wider than a line*, articulated the interconnectedness of the Americas and their shared experiences, such as the recognition of colonial legacies, expressions of the vernacular, the influence of Indigenous understandings, and the relationship to the land.

This summer we are delighted to introduce *SITElines.2018* and its curatorial team—José Luis Blondet, Candice Hopkins, and Ruba Katrib. Working with curatorial advisor Naomi Beckwith, the team has brought together an exhibition featuring the work of twenty-three artists from eight countries. This more limited number of participating artists has allowed for a larger presentation by each, and a significant number of new commissions.

The current iteration of *SITElines* provides an opportunity to reflect on the aspiration of SITE's Americas biennial to embody a vision of collaboration, perspectival diversity, audience and community engagement, and dialogue intended to broaden the lens of contemporary art. Through the experience of *SITElines*, we have been able to test these premises. With the diversity of voices at our curatorial table and in our exhibition spaces, we challenge ourselves and our audience to confront the prejudices and historical amnesia exacted by colonialism and interventionism. Staging presentations that are rigorous, topical, and engaged with urgent issues and ideas that condition our past and our present, we continue to develop new competencies and strategies for collaborative work. *SITElines* tasks us with rethinking labels, stereotypes, and our own biases about art. Its exhibitions have helped us break open the canon of art and expand our shared worldview.

While *SITElines* has ushered in many vital conversations about inclusivity and cultural competency, and has brought fundamental change to our institution, over the past six years we have also witnessed the larger art world's heightened awareness of its own cultural blind spots, colonial histories, and legacies. Art-world news here and abroad exposes a field in need of self-examination and confrontation with the histories of its objects, funders, and collections; we can see the distance even progressive museums still need to go in order to interpret difficult moments in our shared history with culturally sensitive projects and exhibitions.

At the same time, we have seen our field starting to demand equality (equal pay and safe work spaces) and inclusivity (representation and access), and to interrogate power and privilege with questions such as who can speak for whom. While these issues often play out in the public square as sensational art-world news items, at SITE Santa Fe we have sought to live and address them through our institutional culture, actions, and day-to-day commitment to an inclusive vision.

Fortunately, the country as a whole is also becoming more culturally conscious. The mainstream understanding of the publicized protests at Standing Rock, discussions around the interrogation and removal of Confederate monuments, and the rise of the Black Lives Matter movement and other efforts in social justice have all pushed our nation to face the past and reimagine a better and more just future.

Against this cultural and political backdrop we present *Casa tomada* (House taken over), an exhibition that borrows its name and inspiration from a 1946 short story by the Argentine writer Julio Cortázar. First published by Jorge Luis Borges in the literary magazine *Los anales de Buenos Aires*, "Casa tomada" concerns the takeover of an ancestral home by an unseen presence that eventually squeezes out its owners. When the story was written, it had strong resonance in the cultural and political context of Argentina, which was then experiencing the rise of authoritarian power and the fomentation of fear—of change and of "outsiders." *Casa tomada* plays off the tensions and ambiguities of Cortázar's story, addressing the reciprocal and complex relationships among those who arrive, those who remain, and those who are forced out.

Visitors encounter the second touchstone of the exhibition just as they enter the main galleries of *Casa tomada*, where an installation addresses the history of a controversial monument to a sixteenth-century conquistador created in 1993 by the sculptor Reynaldo "Sonny" Rivera. Located in Alcalde in northern New Mexico, the oversize equestrian statue glorifies Juan de Oñate, who took over the region through brutal assault on its people. The installation tells a story of historical trauma more than four centuries old that continues to raise passions in New Mexico today.

It is through this complex lens—of cultural anxiety, of ambiguities of ownership, and of history confronted—that we invite you to experience *Casa tomada*.


Irene Hofmann
Phillips Director and Chief Curator

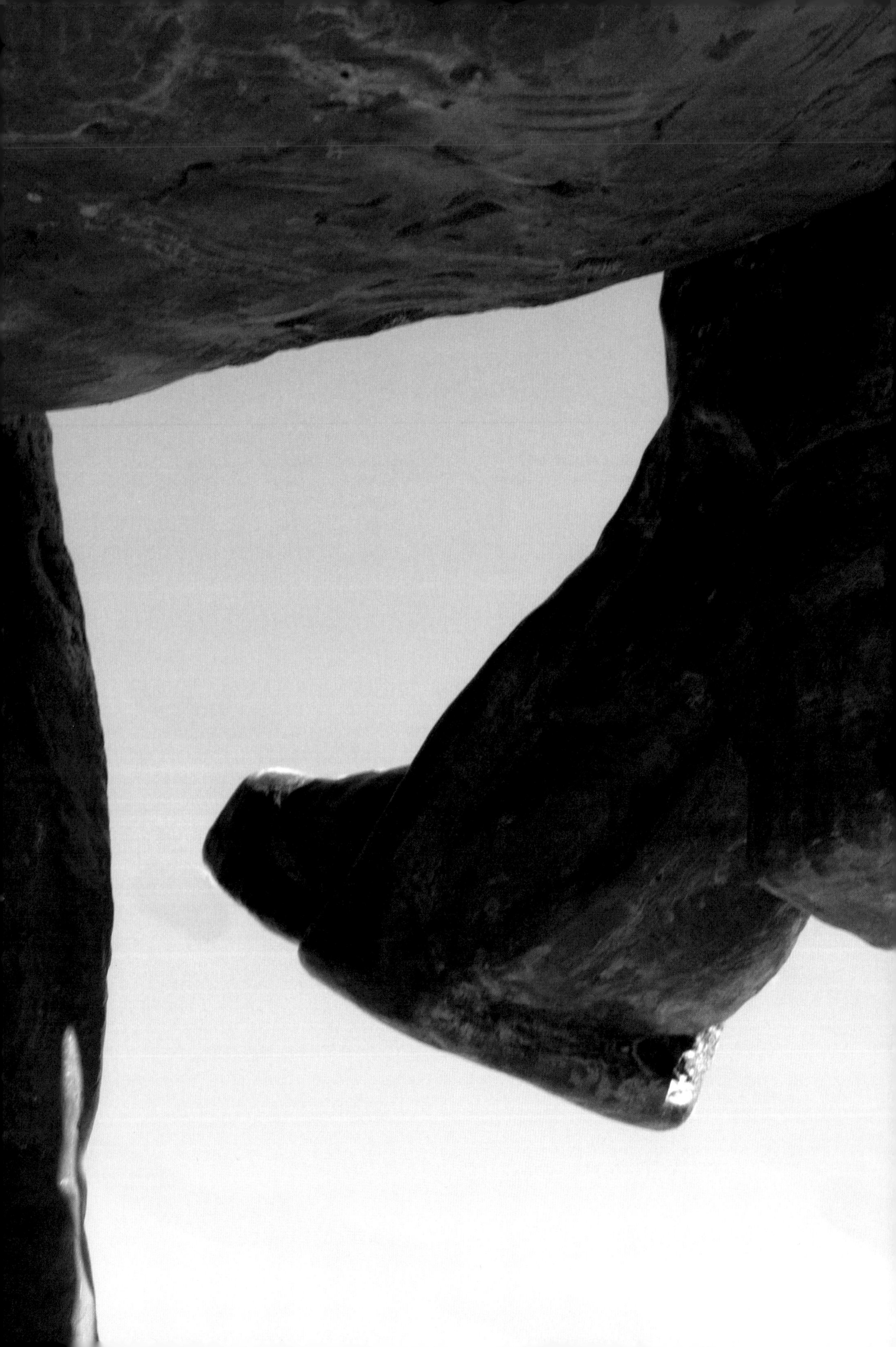

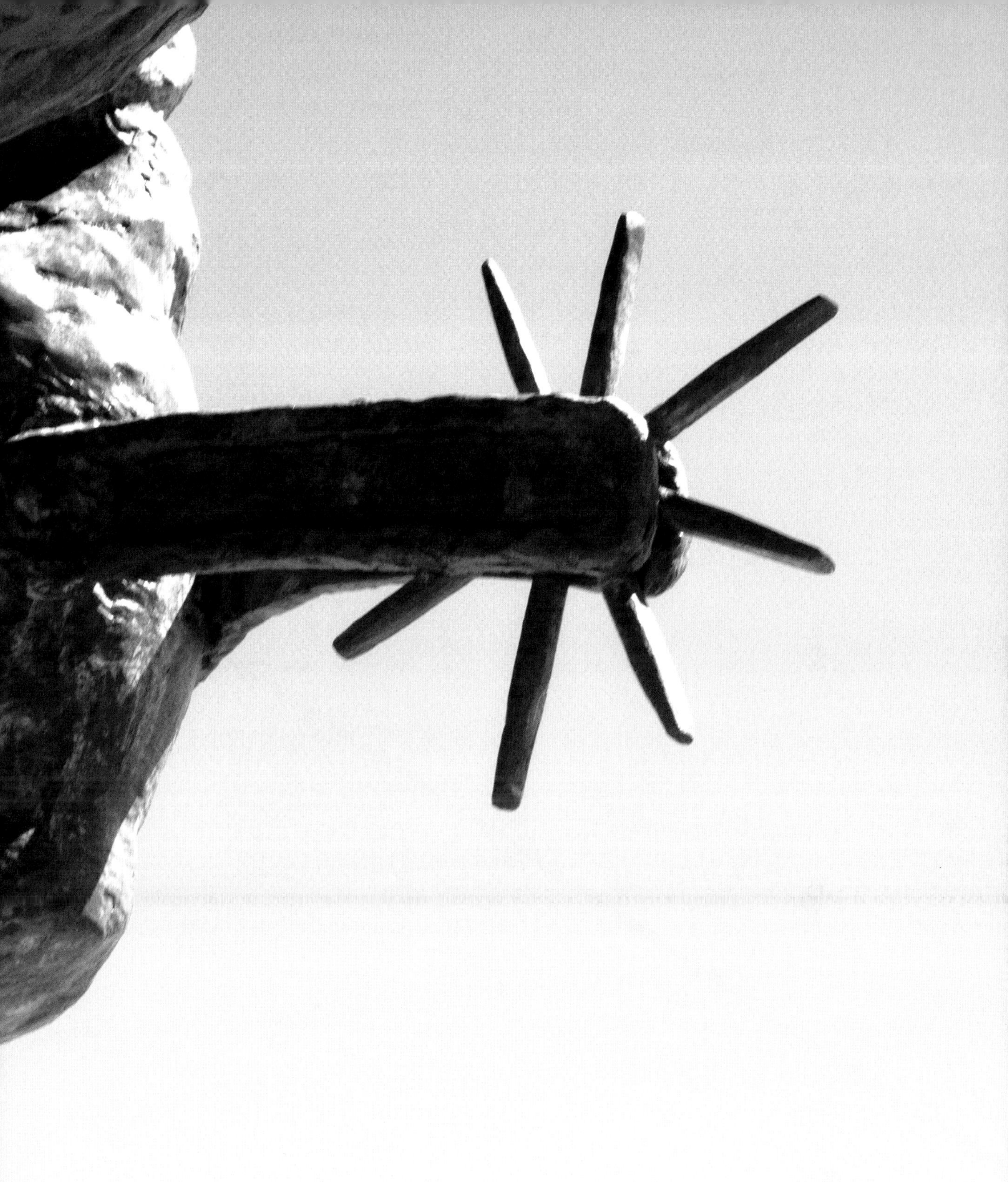

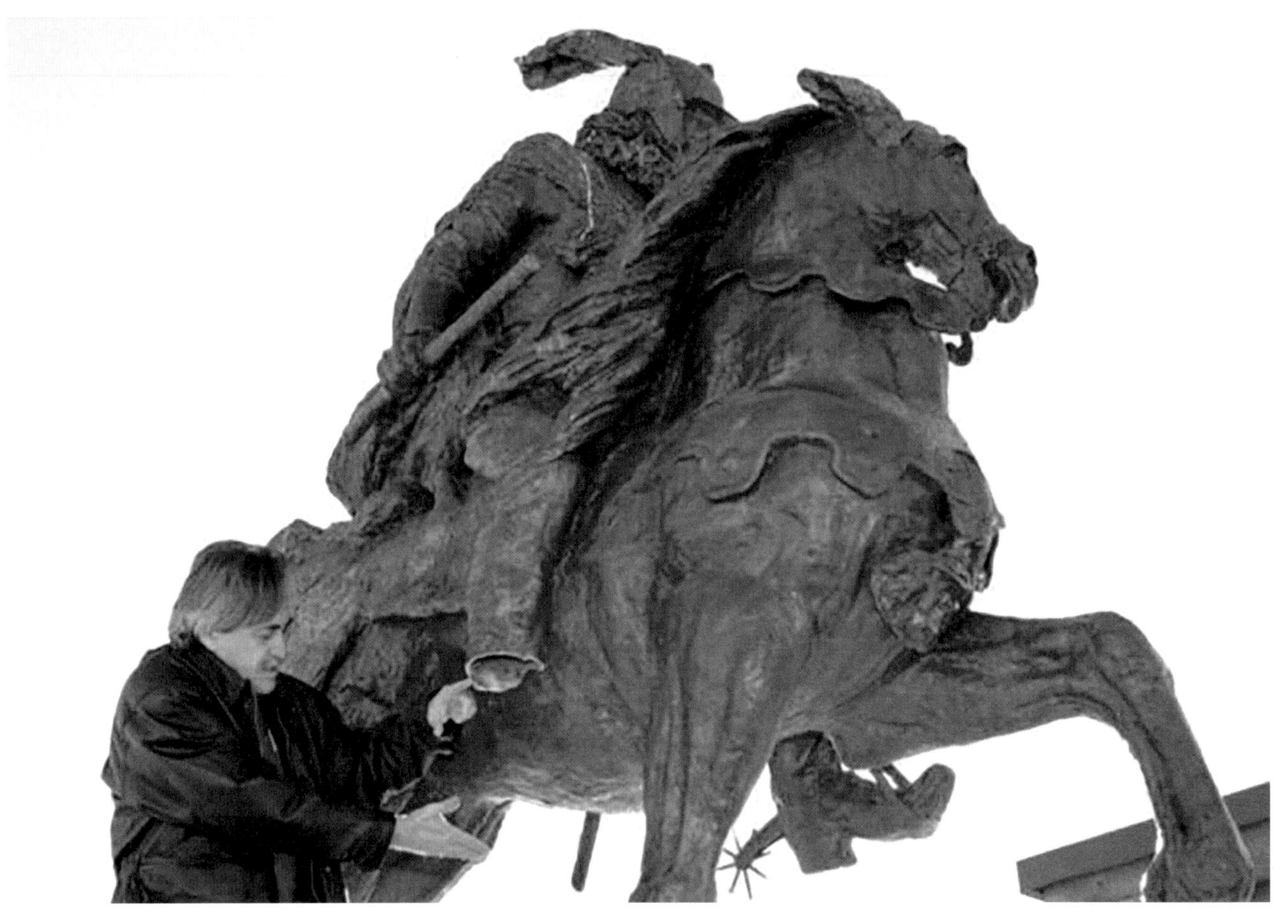

Estevan Arellano, then director of the Oñate Center, poses with the Oñate monument after the foot was removed. The artist who made the statue, Renaldo "Sonny" Rivera, cast a replacement from a mold of the remaining foot. *Albuquerque Journal*. Used with permission

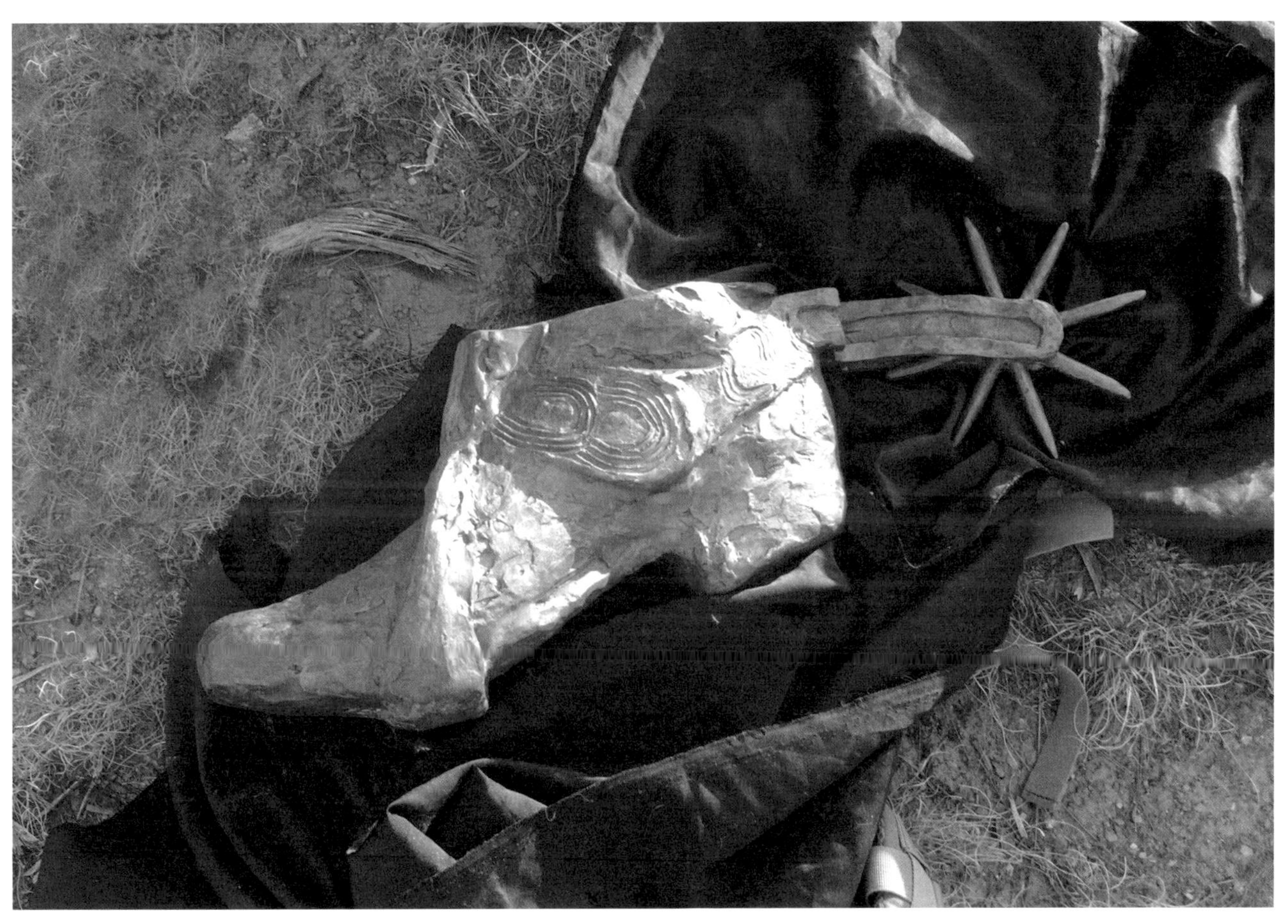

The removed foot of the Oñate monument resurfaced briefly in 2017 when it was shown to filmmaker Chris Eyre and a story appeared in the *New York Times*. Photograph by Chris Eyre

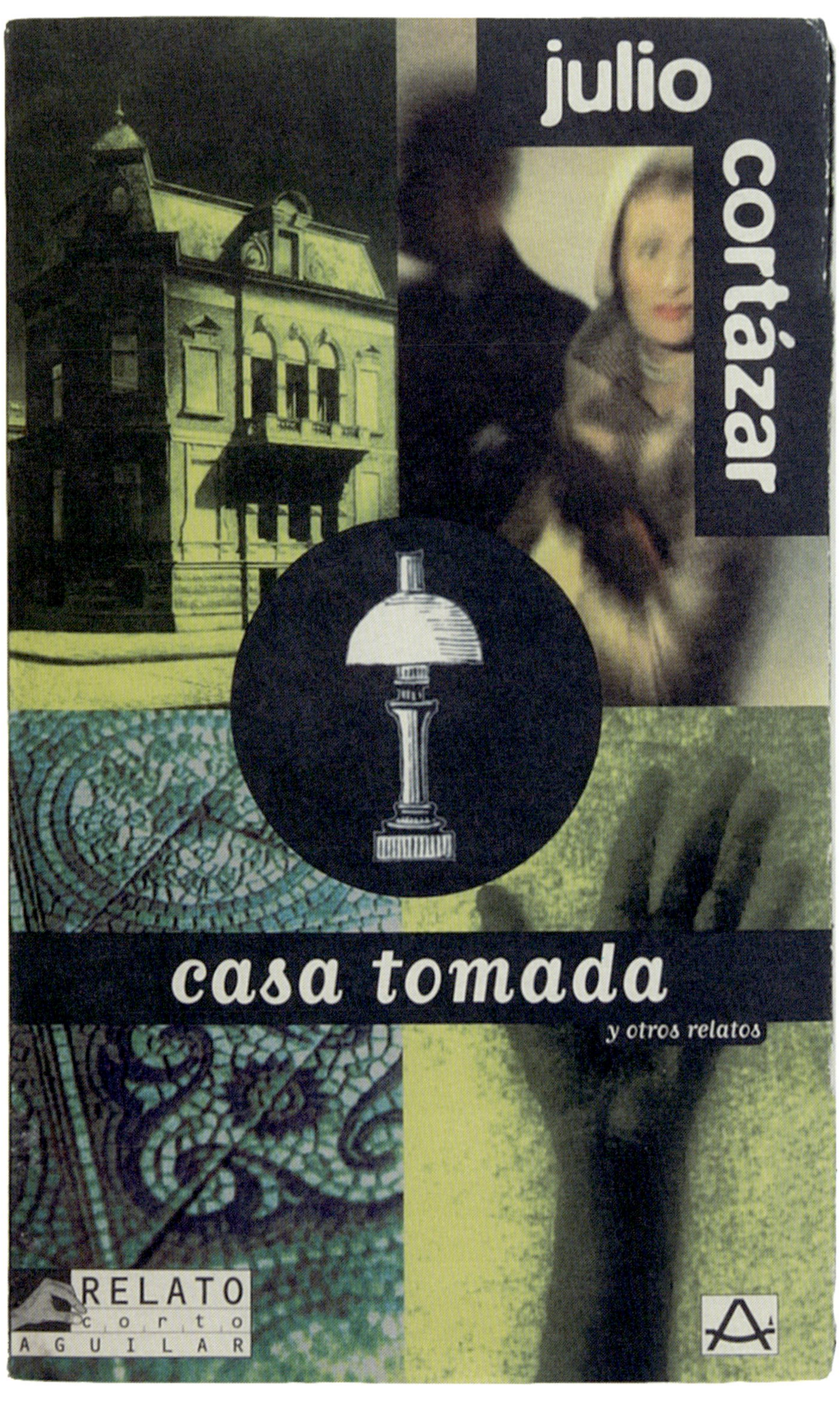


Cover and excerpted pages from Julio Cortázar, *Casa tomada y otros relatos* (Madrid: Aguilar, 1994). Cover design by Alfonso Sostres and graphic design by Rosa Marin

# Casa tomada

 Nos gustaba la casa porque aparte de espaciosa y antigua (hoy que las casas antiguas sucumben a la más ventajosa liquidación de sus materiales) guardaba los recuerdos de nuestros bisabuelos, el abuelo paterno, nuestros padres y toda la infancia.

Nos habituamos Irene y yo a persistir solos en ella, lo que era una locura pues en esa casa podían vivir ocho personas sin estorbarse. Hacíamos la limpieza por la mañana, levantándonos a las siete, y a eso de las once yo le dejaba a Irene las últimas habitaciones por repasar y me iba a la cocina. Almorzábamos a mediodía, siempre puntuales; ya no quedaba nada por hacer fuera de unos pocos platos sucios. Nos resultaba grato almorzar pensando en la casa profunda y silenciosa y cómo nos bastábamos para mantenerla limpia. A veces llegamos a creer que era ella la que no nos dejó casarnos. Irene rechazó dos pretendientes sin mayor motivo, a mí se me murió María Esther antes que llegáramos a comprometernos. Entramos en los cuarenta años con la inexpresada idea de que el nuestro, simple y silencioso matrimonio de hermanos, era necesaria clausura de la genealogía asentada por los bisabuelos en nuestra casa. Nos moriríamos allí algún día, vagos y esquivos primos se quedarían con la casa y la echarían al suelo para enriquecerse con el terreno y los ladrillos; o mejor, nosotros mismos la voltearíamos justicieramente antes de que fuese demasiado tarde.

Irene era una chica nacida para no molestar a nadie. Aparte de su actividad matinal se pasaba el resto del día tejiendo en el sofá de su dormitorio. No sé por qué tejía tanto, yo creo que las mujeres tejen cuando han encontrado en esa labor el gran pretexto para no hacer nada. Irene no era así, tejía cosas siempre necesarias,

tricotas[1] para el invierno, medias para mí, mañanitas[2] y chalecos para ella. A veces tejía un chaleco y después lo destejía en un momento porque algo no le agradaba; era gracioso ver en la canastilla el montón de lana encrespada resistiéndose a perder su forma de algunas horas. Los sábados iba yo al centro a comprarle lana; Irene tenía fe en mi gusto, se complacía con los colores y nunca tuve que devolver madejas. Yo aprovechaba esas salidas para dar una vuelta por las librerías y preguntar vanamente si había novedades en literatura francesa. Desde 1939 no llegaba nada valioso a la Argentina.

Pero es de la casa que me interesa hablar, de la casa y de Irene, porque yo no tengo importancia. Me pregunto qué hubiera hecho Irene sin el tejido. Uno puede releer un libro, pero cuando un pull-over está terminado no se puede repetirlo sin escándalo. Un día encontré el cajón de abajo de la cómoda de alcanfor lleno de pañoletas blancas, verdes, lila. Estaban con naftalina, apiladas como en una mercería; no tuve valor de preguntarle a Irene qué pensaba hacer con ellas. No necesitábamos ganarnos la vida, todos los meses llegaba la plata[3] de los campos y el dinero aumentaba. Pero a Irene solamente la entretenía el tejido, mostraba una destreza maravillosa y a mí se me iban las horas viéndole las manos como erizos plateados, agujas yendo y viniendo y una o dos canastillas en el suelo donde se agitaban constantemente los ovillos. Era hermoso.

1. tricotas: En Argentina, prendas de punto.

2. mañanitas: Prendas de punto femeninas, cortas y abiertas por delante, que ponen encima del camisón.

3. plata: Dinero.

Cómo no acordarme de la distribución de la casa. El comedor, una sala
con gobelinos[4], la biblioteca y tres dormitorios grandes quedaban en
la parte más retirada, la que mira hacia Rodríguez Peña. Solamente un
pasillo con su maciza puerta de roble aislaba esa parte del ala delantera
donde había un baño, la cocina, nuestros dormitorios y el living central,
al cual comunicaban los dormitorios y el pasillo. Se entraba a la casa por
un zaguán con mayólica[5], y la puerta cancel[6] daba al living. De manera
que uno entraba por el zaguán, abría la cancel y pasaba al living; tenía a
los lados las puertas de nuestros dormitorios, y al frente el pasillo que
conducía a la parte más retirada; avanzando por el pasillo se franqueaba
la puerta de roble y más allá empezaba el otro lado de la casa, o bien se
podía girar a la izquierda justamente antes de la puerta y seguir por un
pasillo más estrecho que llevaba a la cocina y el baño. Cuando la puerta
estaba abierta advertía uno que la casa era muy grande; si no, daba la
impresión de un departamento de los que se edifican ahora, apenas para
moverse; Irene y yo vivíamos siempre en esta parte de la casa, casi nunca
íbamos más allá de la puerta de roble, salvo para hacer la limpieza, pues
es increíble cómo se junta tierra en los muebles. Buenos Aires será una
ciudad limpia, pero eso lo debe a sus habitantes y no a otra cosa Hay de-
masiada tierra en el aire, apenas sopla una ráfaga se palpa el polvo en los
mármoles de las consolas y entre los rombos de las carpetas de macramé[7];
da trabajo sacarlo bien con plumero, vuela y se suspende en el aire, un
momento después se deposita de nuevo en los muebles y los pianos.

Lo recordaré siempre con claridad porque fue simple y sin circunstan-
cias inútiles. Irene estaba tejiendo en su dormitorio, eran las ocho de la
noche y de repente se me ocurrió poner al fuego la pavita[8] del mate[9]. Fui

4. gobelinos: Tapices. El término proviene de la fábrica de tapices fundada en Francia
   por Enrique IV en 1601.
5. mayólica: Loza con esmalte metálico.
6. cancel: Contrapuerta de tres hojas, una de frente y dos laterales cerradas por un techo.
   Suele adosarse a la puerta principal para evitar corrientes.
7. macramé: Tejido en forma de redecilla hecho a mano. Suele emplearse en decoración.
8. pavita: Tetera para preparar el mate
9. mate: Infusión de hojas de hierba preparada con agua y azúcar

por el pasillo hasta enfrentar la entornada puerta de roble, y daba la vuelta al codo que llevaba a la cocina cuando escuché algo en el comedor o la biblioteca. El sonido venia impreciso y sordo, como un volcarse de silla sobre la alfombra o un ahogado susurro de conversación. También lo oí, al mismo tiempo o un segundo después, en el fondo del pasillo que traía desde aquellas piezas hasta la puerta. Me tiré contra la puerca antes de que fuera demasiado tarde, la cerré de golpe apoyando el cuerpo; felizmente la llave escaba puesta de nuestro lado y además corrí el gran cerrojo para más seguridad.

Fui a la cocina, calenté: la pavita, y cuando estuve de vuelta con la bandeja del mate le dije a Irene:

-Tuve que cerrar la puerca del pasillo. Han tomado la parte del fondo.

Dejó caer el tejido y me miró con sus graves ojos cansados.

-¿Estás seguro?

Asentí.

-Entonces -dijo recogiendo las agujas ten dremos que vivir en este lado.

Yo cebaba[10] el mate con mucho cuidado, pero ella tardó un rato en reanudar su labor. Me acuerdo que tejía un chaleco gris; a mí me gustaba ese chaleco.

Los primeros días nos pareció penoso porque ambos habíamos dejado en la parte tomada muchas cosas que queríamos. Mis libros de literatura francesa, por ejemplo, estaban todos en la biblioteca. Irene extrañaba unas carpetas, un par de pantuflas que tanto la abrigaban en invierno. Yo sentía mi pipa de enebro y creo que Irene pensó en una botella de Hesperidina[11] de muchos años. Con frecuencia (pero esto solamente

10. cebaba: De cebar, preparar el mate con agua caliente para tomarlo.
11. Hesperidina: Sustancia cuyo componente es la glucosa obtenida de
    la piel de los citricos.

sucedió los primeros días) cerrábamos algún cajón de las cómodas y nos mirábamos con tristeza.

-No está aquí.

Y era una cosa mas de todo lo que habíamos perdido al otro lado de la casa.

Pero también tuvimos ventajas. La limpieza se simplificó tanto que aun levantándose tardísimo, a las nueve y media por ejemplo, no daban las once y ya estábamos de brazos cruzados. Irene se acostumbró a ir conmigo a la cocina y ayudarme a preparar el almuerzo. Lo pensamos bien, y se decidió esto: mientras yo preparaba el almuerzo, Irene cocinaría platos para comer fríos de noche. Nos alegramos porque siempre resulta molesto tener que abandonar los dormitorios al atardecer y ponerse a cocinar. Ahora nos bastaba con la mesa en el dormitorio de Irene y las fuentes de comida fiambre.

Irene estaba contenta porque le quedaba más tiempo para tejer. Yo andaba un poco perdido a causa de los libros, pero por no afligir a mi hermana me puse a revisar la colección de escampillas[12] de papá, y eso me sirvió para matar el tiempo. Nos divertíamos mucho, cada uno en sus cosas, casi siempre reunidos en el dormitorio de Irene que era más cómodo. A veces Irene decía:

-Fíjate este punto que se me ha ocurrido. ¿No da un dibujo de trébol?

Un rato después era yo el que le ponía ante los ojos un cuadradito de papel para que viese el mérito de algún sello de Eupen y Malmedy[13]. Estábamos bien, y poco a poco empezábamos a no pensar. Se puede vivir sin pensar.

---

12. estampillas: Sellos de correos.
13. Eupen y Malmédy: Municipios de la provincia de Lieja (Bélgica).

(Cuando Irene soñaba en alta voz yo me desvelaba enseguida. Nunca pude habituarme a esa voz de estatua o papagayo, voz que viene de los sueños y no de la garganta. Irene decía que mis sueños consistían en grandes sacudones que a veces hacían caer el cobertor. Nuestros dormitorios tenían el living de por medio, pero de noche se escuchaba cualquier cosa en la casa. Nos oíamos respirar, toser, presentíamos el ademám que conduce a la llave del velador, los mutuos y frecuentes insomnios.

Aparte de eso todo estaba callado en la casa. De día eran los rumores domésticos, el roce metálico de las agujas de tejer, un crujido al pasar las hojas del álbum filatélico. La puerta de roble, creo haberlo dicho, era maciza. En la cocina y el baño, que quedaban tocando la parte tomada, nos poníamos a hablar en voz más alta o Irene cantaba canciones de cuna. En una cocina hay demasiado ruido de loza y vidrios para que otros sonidos irrumpan en ella. Muy pocas veces permitíamos allí el silencio, pero cuando tornábamos a los dormitorios y al living, entonces la casa se ponía callada y a media luz, hasta pisábamos más despacio para no molestarnos. Yo creo que era por eso que de noche, cuando Irene empezaba a soñar en alca voz, me desvelaba enseguida)

Es casi repetir lo mismo salvo las consecuencias. De noche siento sed, y antes de acostarnos le dije a Irene que iba hasta la cocina a servirme un vaso de agua. Desde la puerta del dormitorio (ella tejía) oí el ruido en la cocina; tal vez en la cocina o cal vez en el baño porque el codo del pasillo apagaba el sonido. A Irene le llamó la atención mi brusca manera de detenerme, y vino a mi lado sin decir palabra. Nos quedamos escuchando los ruidos, notando claramente que eran de este lado de la puerta de roble, en la cocina y en el baño, o en el pasillo mismo donde empezaba el codo casi al lado nuestro.

No nos miramos siquiera. Apreté el brazo de Irene y la hice correr conmigo hasta la puerta cancel, sin volvemos hacia atrás. Los ruidos se oían más fuerte pero siempre sordos a espaldas nuestras. Cerré de un golpe la cancel y nos quedamos en el zaguán. Ahora no se oía nada

-Han tornado esta parte -dijo Irene. El tejido le colgaba de las manos y las hebras iban hasta la cancel y se perdían debajo. Cuando vio que los ovillos habían quedado del otro lado soltó el tejido sin mirarlo.

-¿Tuviste tiempo de traer alguna cosa? -  le pregunte inútilmente.

-No, nada.

Estábamos con lo puesto. Me acordé de los quince mil pesos en el armario de mi dormitorio. Ya era tarde ahora.

Como me quedaba el reloj pulsera, vi que eran las once de la noche. Rodeé con mi brazo la cintura de Irene (yo creo que ella estaba llorando) y salimos a la calle. Antes de alejamos tuve lástima, cerré bien la puerta de entrada y tiré la llave a la alcantarilla. No fuese que a algún pobre diablo se le ocurriera robar y se metiera en la casa, a esa hora y con la casa tomada.

# HOUSE TAKEN OVER

Julio Cortázar

*We liked the house because, apart from its being old and spacious (in a day when old houses go down for a profitable auction of their construction materials), it kept the memories of great-grandparents, our paternal grandfather, our parents and the whole of childhood.*

*Irene and I got used to staying in the house by ourselves, which was crazy, eight people could have lived in that place and not have gotten in each other's way. We rose at seven in the morning and got the cleaning done, and about eleven I left Irene to finish off whatever rooms and went to the kitchen. We lunched at noon precisely; then there was nothing left to do but a few dirty plates. It was pleasant to take lunch and commune with the great hollow, silent house, and it was enough for us just to keep it clean. We ended up thinking, at times, that that was what had kept us from marrying. Irene turned down two suitors for no particular reason, and María Esther went and died on me before we could manage to get engaged. We were easing into our forties with the unvoiced concept that the quiet, simple marriage of sister and brother was the indispensable end to a line established in this house by our grandparents. We would die here someday, obscure and distant cousins would inherit the place, have it torn down, sell the bricks and get rich on the building plot; or more justly and better yet, we would topple it ourselves before it was too late.*

*Irene never bothered anyone. Once the morning housework was finished, she spent the rest of the day on the sofa in her bedroom, knitting. I couldn't tell you why she knitted so much; I think women knit when they discover that it's a fat excuse to do nothing at all. But Irene was not like that, she always knitted necessities, sweaters for winter, socks for me, handy morning robes and bedjackets for herself. Sometimes she would do a jacket, then unravel it the next moment because there was something that didn't please her; it was pleasant to see a pile of tangled wool in her knitting basket fighting a losing battle for a few hours to retain its shape. Saturdays I went downtown to buy wool; Irene had faith in my good taste, was pleased with the colors and never a skein had to be returned. I took advantage of these trips to make the rounds of the bookstores, uselessly asking if they had anything new in French literature. Nothing worthwhile had arrived in Argentina since 1939.*

*But it's the house I want to talk about, the house and Irene, I'm not very important. I wonder what Irene would have done without her knitting. One can reread a book, but once a pullover is finished you can't do it over again, it's some kind of disgrace. One day I found that the drawer at the bottom of the chiffonier, replete with mothballs, was filled with shawls, white, green, lilac. Stacked amid a great smell of camphor— it was like a shop; I didn't have the nerve to ask her what she planned to do with them. We didn't have to earn our living, there was plenty coming in from the farms each month, even piling up.  But Irene was only interested in the knitting and showed a wonderful dexterity, and for me the hours slipped away watching her, her hands like silver sea-urchins, needles flashing, and one or two knitting baskets on the floor, the balls of yarn jumping about. It was lovely.*

*How not to remember the layout of that house. The dinning room, a living room with tapestries, the library and three large bedrooms in the section most recessed, the one that faced toward Rodríguez Peña. Only a corridor with its massive oak door separated that part from the front wing, where there was a bath, the kitchen, our bedrooms and the hall. One entered the house through a vestibule with enameled tiles, and a wrought-iron grated door opened onto the living room. You had to come in through the vestibule and open the gate to go into the living room; the doors to our bedrooms were on either side of this, and opposite it was the corridor leading to the back section; going down the passage, one swung open the oak door beyond which was the other part of the house; or just before the door, one could turn to the left and go down a narrower passageway which led to the kitchen and the bath. When the door was open, you became aware of the size of the house; when it was closed, you had the impression of an apartment, like the ones they build today, with barely enough room to move around in. Irene and I always lived in this part of the house and hardly ever went beyond the oak door except to do the cleaning. Incredible how much dust collected on the furniture. It may be Buenos Aires is a clean city, but she owes it to her population and nothing else. There's too much dust in the air, the slightest breeze and it's back on the marble console tops and in the diamond patterns of the tooled-leather desk set. It's a lot of work to get it off with a feather duster; the motes rise and hang in the air, and settle again a minute later on the pianos and the furniture.*

*I'll always have a clear memory of it because it happened so simply and without fuss. Irene was knitting in her bedroom, it was eight at night, and I suddenly decided to put the water up for mate. I went down the corridor as far as the oak door, which was ajar, then turned into the hall toward the kitchen, when I heard something in the library or the dining room. The sound came through muted and indistinct, a chair being knocked over onto the carpet or the muffled buzzing of a conversation. At the same time or a second later, I heard it at the end of the passage which led from those two rooms toward the door. I hurled myself against the door before it was too late and shut it, leaned on it with the weight of my body; luckily, the key was on our side; moreover, I ran the great bolt into place, just to be safe.*

*I went down to the kitchen, heated the kettle, and when I got back with the tray of mate, I told Irene:*

*"I had to shut the door to the passage. They've taken over the back part."*

*She let her knitting fall and looked at me with her tired, serious eyes.*

*"You're sure?"*

*I nodded.*

*"In that case," she said, picking up her needles again, "we'll have to live on this side."*

*I sipped at the mate very carefully, but she took her time starting her work again. I remember it was a grey vest she was knitting. I liked that vest.*

*The first few days were painful, since we'd both left so many things in the part that had been taken over. My collection of French literature, for example, was still in the library. Irene had left several folios of stationery and a pair of slippers that she used a lot in the winter. I missed my briar pipe, and Irene, I think, regretted the loss of an ancient bottle of Hesperidin. It happened repeatedly (but only in the first few days) that we would close some drawer or cabinet and look at one another sadly.*

*"It's not here."*

*One thing more among the many lost on the other side of the house.*

*But there were advantages, too. The cleaning was so much simplified that, even when we got up late, nine thirty for instance, by eleven we were sitting around with our arms folded.*

*Irene got into the habit of coming to the kitchen with me to help get lunch. We thought about it and decided on this: while I prepared the lunch, Irene would cook up dishes that could be eaten cold in the evening. We were happy with the arrangement because it was always such a bother to have to leave our bedrooms in the evening and start to cook. Now we made do with the table in Irene's room and platters of cold supper.*

*Since it left her more time for knitting, Irene was content. I was a little lost without my books, but so as not to inflict myself on my sister, I set about reordering papa's stamp collection; that killed some time. We amused ourselves sufficiently, each with his own thing, almost always getting together in Irene's bedroom, which was the more comfortable. Every once in a while, Irene might say:*

*"Look at this pattern I just figured out, doesn't it look like clover?"*

*After a bit it was I, pushing a small square of paper in front of her so that she could see the excellence of some stamp or another from Eupen-et-Malmédy. We were fine, and little by little we stopped thinking. You can live without thinking.*

*Whenever Irene talked in her sleep, I woke up immediately and stayed awake. I never could get used to this voice from a statue or a parrot, a voice that came out of the dreams, not from a throat. Irene said that in my sleep I flailed about enormously and shook the blankets off. We had the living room between us, but at night you could hear everything in the house. We heard each other breathing, coughing, could even feel each other reaching for the light switch when, as happened frequently, neither of us could fall asleep.*

*Aside from our nocturnal rumblings, everything was quiet in the house. During the day there were the household sounds, the metallic click of knitting needles, the rustle of stamp-album pages turning. The oak door was massive, I think I  said that. In the kitchen or the bath, which adjoined the part that was taken over, we managed to talk loudly, or Irene sang lullabies. In a kitchen there's always too much noise, the plates and glasses, for there to be interruptions from other sounds. We seldom allowed our-selves silence there, but when we went back to our rooms or to the living room, then the house grew quiet, half-lit, we ended by stepping around more slowly so as not to disturb one another. I think it was because of this that I woke up irremediably and at once when Irene began to talk in her sleep.*

*Except for the consequences, it's nearly a matter of repeating the same scene over again. I was thirsty that night, and before we went to sleep, I told Irene that I was going to the kitchen for a glass of water. From the door of the bedroom (she was knitting) I heard the noise in the kitchen; if not the kitchen, then the bath, the passage off at that angle dulled the sound. Irene noticed how brusquely I had paused, and came up beside me without a word. We stood listening to the noises, growing more and more sure that they were on our side of the oak door, if not the kitchen then the bath, or in the hall itself at the turn, almost next to us.*

*We didn't wait to look at one another. I took Irene's arm and forced her to run with me to the wrought-iron door, not waiting to look back. You could hear the noises, still muffled but louder, just behind us. I slammed the grating and we stopped in the vestibule. Now there was nothing to be heard.*

*"They've taken over our section," Irene said. The knitting had reeled off from her hands and the yarn ran back toward the door and disappeared under it. When she saw that the balls of yarn were on the other side, she dropped the knitting without looking at it.*

*"Did you have time to bring anything?" I asked hopelessly.*

*"No, nothing."*

*We had what we had on. I remembered fifteen thousand pesos in the wardrobe in my bedroom. Too late now.*

*I still had my wristwatch on and saw that it was 11 P.M.  I took Irene around the waist (I think she was crying) and that was how we went into the street. Before we left, I felt terrible; I locked the front door up tight and tossed the key down the sewer. It wouldn't do to have some poor devil decide to go in and rob the house, at that hour and with the house taken over.*

Reprinted from Julio Cortázar, *Blow-Up and Other Stories*, trans. Paul Blackburn (New York: Pantheon, 1985)

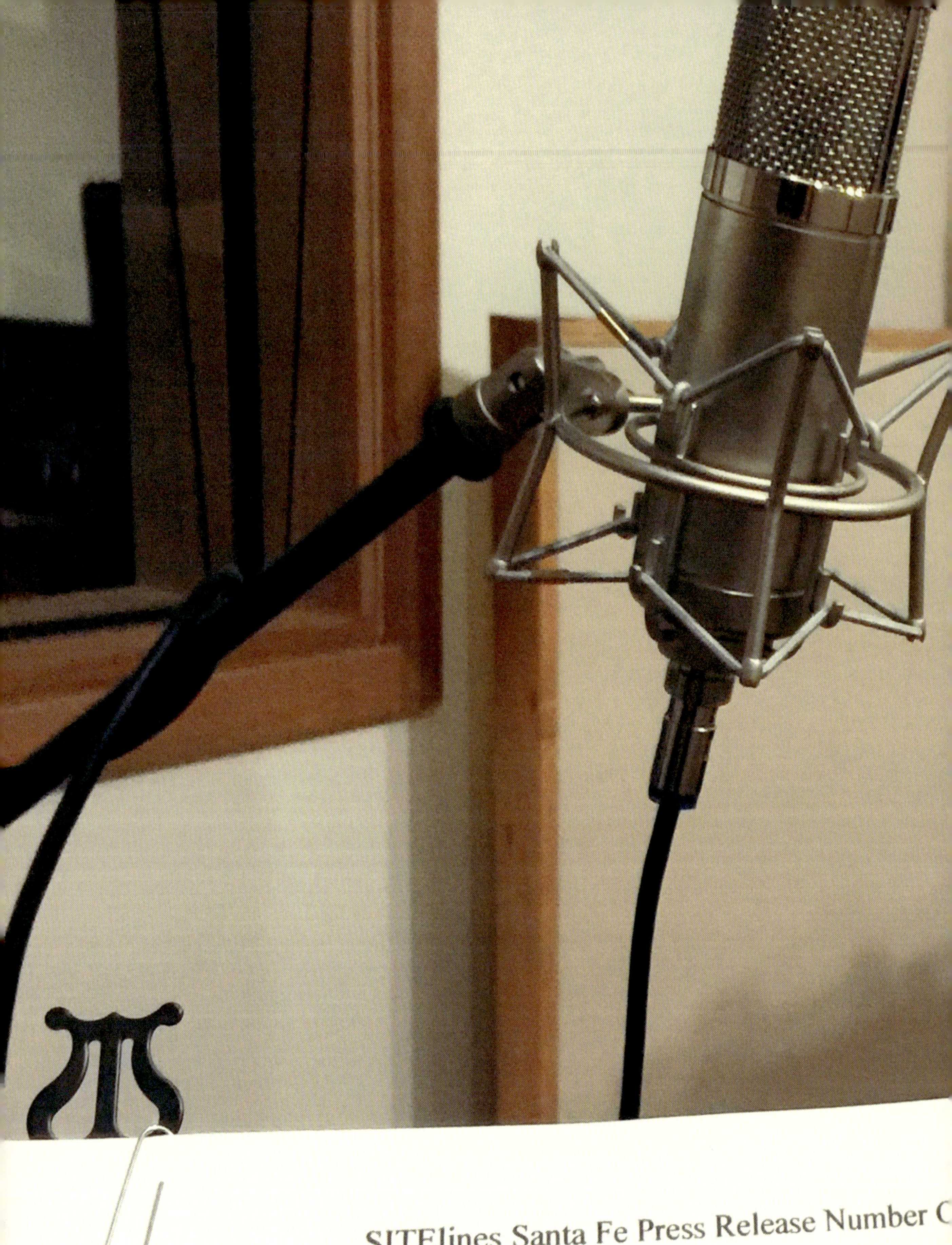
SITElines Santa Fe Press Release Number O
Voice 2
Soprano 1
SITE - lines San - ta Fe Press Re - lease Nu - mber one

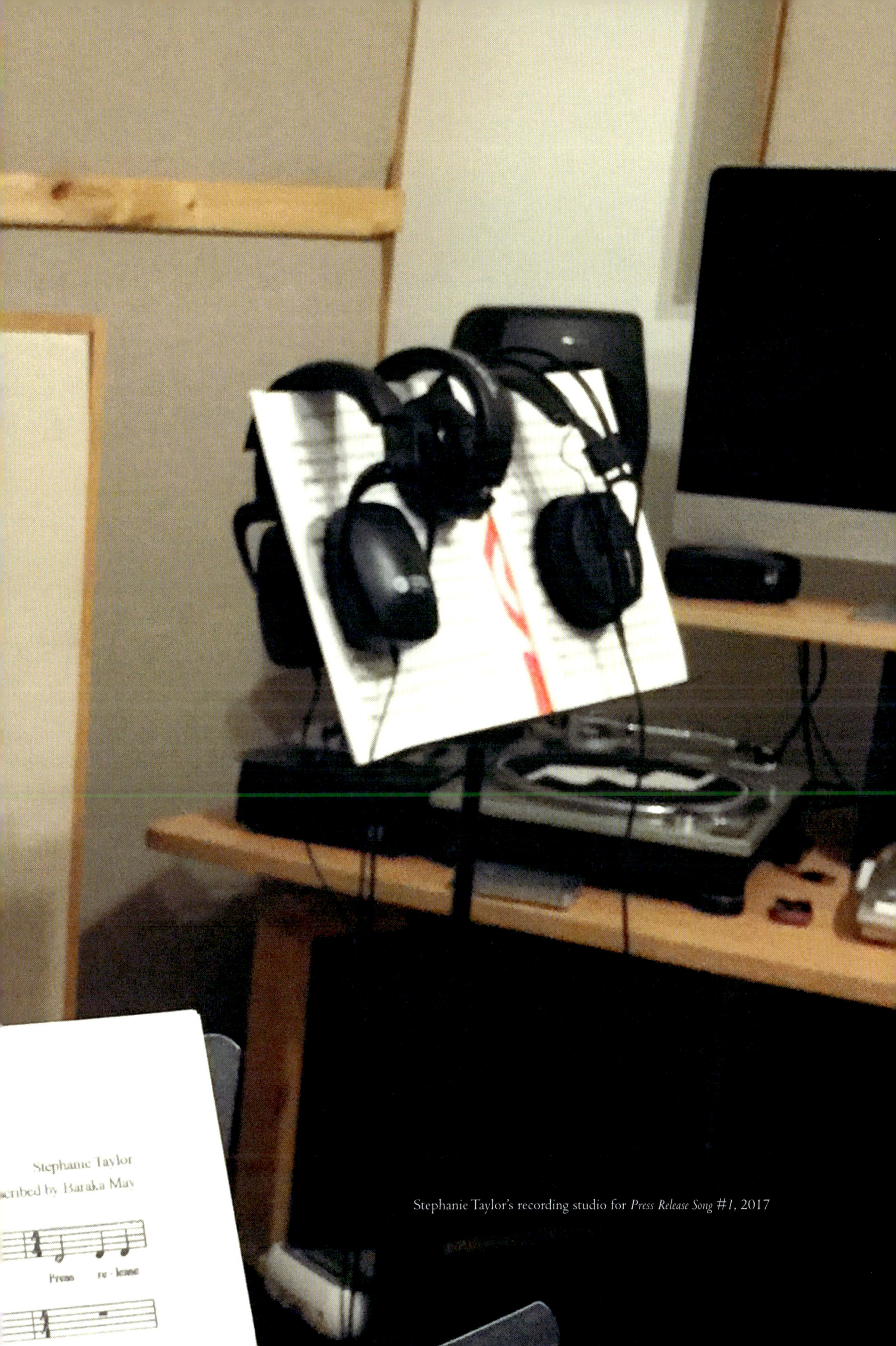


Stephanie Taylor's recording studio for *Press Release Song #1*, 2017

# LOCKED OUT (GHOSTS AND ORTHOPEDICS)

José Luis Blondet

Opening one's home to strangers can be seen as a gesture of comfort and ease, or an invitation to catastrophe. Ranging from the luminous to the ominous, the word *hospitality* houses dynamics of power defined by the roles of owner and user, host and guest—or migrant, invader, perpetrator, interloper, ghost, or visitor from the past. It is hard to think of a less inviting, less hospitable, way to start this essay than by quoting Jacques Derrida on the laws of hospitality, but the following provides a useful shortcut in explaining the contradictory and volatile nature of a concept that appears intermittently, sometimes as a specter, throughout the exhibition *Casa tomada*. It serves also as a reminder of the harshness implicit in this transaction:

> So it is indeed the master, the one who invites, the inviting host, who becomes the hostage—and who really always has been. And the guest, the invited hostage, becomes the one who invites the one who invites, the master of the host. The guest becomes the host's host. The guest (hôte) becomes the host (hôte) of the host (hôte). These substitutions make everyone into everyone else's hostage.[1]

The perversity of hospitality is a central aspect of "Casa tomada," the unresolved and unresolvable tale of dispossession and class by Julio Cortázar that lends its name to the exhibition. In the story, a sister and brother are gradually pushed out of their family home. The house is not divided but invaded by forces that do not withdraw. The siblings modify their daily routines to keep living in the sections of the property that are still available to them. But the implacable occupation advances until the siblings are forced out to the sidewalk with nothing but a wristwatch and key. They lock themselves out of their own home and throw the key in the sewer.

The decision to name the biennial using the story's original foreign-language title stresses the taking over of the familiar: *tomada* evinces a military operation, a supernatural takeover, an alienation of place. Several of the artists represented contest notions of belonging— one's belonging to a place, or a place belonging to oneself—while raising timely questions about what constitutes a shelter, a refuge, a hospice. And, more boldly, who and what is a foreigner.

Dispossession dictates the mood of Victor Estrada's paintings. Their charming titles (*Big Rock Candy Mountain*, *Flowering Tree*, or *Pink Cloud*) rarely coincide with their spectral quality. Layers of glazing, drippings, and articulation produce images of a place that is almost not there. The landscape is not host but ghost. No bodies inhabit it, only outgrowths, organs, and amputated parts that appear as cutouts against a fleshy backdrop. In *I Went Walking and She Threw Me a Look / aka "Froggies Went a Courtin"*, 2017, the foot of a white man is planted at dead center, under an expansive baby-blue sky. An incongruous ceramic pot with a detailed floral motif commonly seen in border towns rests on the ground in front of a cat or raccoon that at first does not look out of proportion. A dark brown sun shines.

Borders and the border are recurrent motifs in Estrada's work, where everything is in transit but nothing moves. Clouds, trees, occasional patches of grass, and slurries of color suggest a landscape but, in many cases, it is hard to determine if the figures are outdoors or indoors, home or exiled. In *The Spirit of the Living and the Dead and Cotton Candy/Posada*, 2017, a flaccid, amputated tongue hangs down. A skull that has donned a ridiculous white wig hovers over a tiny flat door superimposed on the painting, which doesn't seem to take you anywhere, or offer a way out. Or a way in. An illusionistic and useless threshold inserted to disorient.

The Kawésqar, one of the three aboriginal groups who inhabited western Patagonia, first made their life nomadically, canoeing across the vast archipelago. But a long and infamous history of exploitation, land grabs, imported disease, and exoticism decimated them to the verge of extinction.[2] In the early 1930s, due to the erratic politics of the Chilean government, the surviving Kawésqar were confined to a sedentary life.[3] In 1994, Paz Errázuriz embarked on an eight-year project to photograph the few full-blooded Kawésqar remaining in Tierra del Fuego (fewer than thirty people, the artist recounts), partially to debunk the myth of their disappearance. She titled the resulting series *Nomads of the Sea* after the important anthropological, linguistic, and geographical study published in 1955 by Joseph Emperaire (1912–1958), a researcher affiliated with the Musée de l'Homme in Paris. Another ethnographer, the Austrian missionary Martin Gusinde (1886–1969), traveled to research and photograph the Kawésqar, Selk'nam, and Yagán between 1918 and 1924, producing an important though disputed visual legacy of these cultures. Considering the timing of *Nomads of the Sea*, whose preparation took place during the first years of democracy after the Pinochet regime, the project can be read as the inscription of the surviving Kawésqar in the newly regained democratic state,[4] freed from the scientific and ethnographic gaze: "Paz Errázuriz repeats Emperarire's itinerary not to illustrate a classic work of ethnography but to construct her autobiography."[5]

At the other end of South America, the
Tower of David in Caracas is a vast high-rise
building that was taken over by thousands of
people in a case of squatting that has become
emblematic, mainly for the political rhetoric
fabricated to feed the myth of revolution and
the redistribution of wealth in Venezuela.
Squatting is not a violation of the rules of
hospitality but its very definition. In principle,
there is no role-switching in this case, since
the hosting part of the equation is lacking
and the uninvited guests move in to make the
house their own. The tale's allure is irresistible,
reminiscent of Bertolt Brecht's *Threepenny Opera*
("What is the robbing of a bank compared to
the founding of a bank?"). The skeleton of an
unfinished bank tower in the city's downtown
stood empty for more than ten years after the
unexpected passing of its main investor and
promoter, David Brillembourg, in 1993; its
biblical-sounding name is a reference to this
"creator." Squatting began within the building
in 2007, and by 2010 one of the largest vertical
slums in Latin America was in full bloom.
Beauty parlors, day care centers, bodegas, and
a very tight set of rules and codes of conduct
were overseen by an ex-convict in charge of
this ideal self-made community, drug cartel,
paradigm of the revolution, or fabulous cast
of misery-porn actors broadcast on TV and
in the international media.

For their project on the Tower, Ángela Bonadies
and Juan José Olavarría met with El Niño, the
absolute capo of the building, in the parking
lot that functioned as his office. In anticipation
of their meeting, they had prepared hypothetical
scenarios for negotiating access to the Tower,
but, to their surprise, the meeting was brief,
with only a few words exchanged before he
granted them access. Once inside the Tower,
the artists forged alliances with the inhabitants
they photographed, from the families who let
them into their apartments to the hairdresser
who spoke in code about the frightening
homophobia in the community. Moving away
from the strategies of traditional photographic
documentation, Bonadies and Olavarría used
transitional spaces—doorways, corridors,
common patios—to address the clashing of
architectures and cultures,[6] noting the failures
of each model, instead of insisting on the
relevant but abused litany of the broken
promises of modernism in Latin America.

The artists elaborate on their role as intruders
in the life of the squatters in a script for the
performance piece *In the Bowels of the Beast*, 2014,
while also highlighting the power dynamic
established in the Tower far beyond the utopic
reading of this taking over:

*A: left-wing / right-wing / the same shit, la
misma mierda*

*J: you rude thing! the beast speaks not of wings but
of power, the power of the side, the side she's on:
that's the side, power, the beast is power, she has no
wings but greed*

*A: and the beast learns, she goes through a learning
process and has learnt to shatter language to work
her way*[7]

Glancing over the intertwined timelines of squatting in the Tower and the rise to power of Hugo Chávez, then president of the country and leader of what he called the Bolivarian Revolution, suggests additional allegorical layers in this problematic *casa tomada*:

*1989- A violent social protest erupts in Caracas and neighboring towns, motivated by the government's economic reforms and the rise of gasoline and public transportation costs. The government, under the democratically elected President Carlos Andrés Pérez, brutally represses the protests and riots in what becomes known as the Caracazo.*

*1990- Construction of the Tower of David, funded by investor David Brillembourg, begins.*

*1992- Army Lieutenant Hugo Chávez attempts a coup d'état against Pérez. Failing, he surrenders in a televised broadcast.*

*1993- Brillembourg dies and construction of the Tower is halted*

*1994- Former president Rafael Caldera wins the democratic election, and pardons Chávez.*

*1999- Chávez wins the democratic election. The Inter-American Court of Human Rights finds that the Pérez government committed violations of human rights during the Caracazo, including extrajudicial killings.*

*2007- Over two hundred families take over the Tower of David.*

*2013- The rumored passing of Chávez is officially announced by Vice-President Nicolás Maduro, who replaces him.*

*2014- Maduro's government announces a plan to evict the squatters from the Tower following a deal with the Chinese government to take possession of the property.*

*2015- The last squatters are evicted from the Tower.*

*2018- The Tower remains an empty and unfinished ruin.*

Inherently, foundational myths establish the terms under which a community will understand and imagine their place of origin— the rules of conduct and a way around them. The point of departure for Naufus Ramírez-Figueroa's installation is an episode from Book I of *Popol Vuh*, a Mayan creation book that reflects the cosmological vision of the K'iche' people. In their second attempt to create human beings, deities employ wood. Unlike their mud creatures, who could not talk, the wooden humans are able to speak, but they do not have feelings and do not praise or show gratitude to their creators. They are destroyed by floods and fires. Several run into the jungle to save their lives and become monkeys (explaining the similarity of the species), while those who run to their houses are violently attacked by pots, pans, tortilla grinders, and other utensils, which turn against them to protest their ingratitude.

Ramírez-Figueroa's installation consists of a large mobile from which pots and plates loosely inspired by archaeological Mayan finds hang. Along with the affective images of hospitality and retaliation provided by *Popol Vuh*, Ramírez-Figueroa has included a few stereotypically French-looking vases and jars to evoke the story of Los Altos, a short-lived independent state that separated from Guatemala in 1838. The *altenses* embraced the *mode française* in ornamentation, a gesture the artist interprets as their effort to mold an identity far removed from that of their immediate neighbors of Guatemala and Mexico. The juxtaposition of these contrasting objects adds a spin to the mobile's sense of balance and counterbalance. Contrary to the mute house in the Cortázar story, the home of the wooden men talks back to demand appreciation and attention. The props take over and destroy the master.

Who are you? How do you say your name? Accents, misunderstandings, and legibility are central to the two projects by Stephanie Taylor commissioned for *Casa tomada*. Borrowing SITE Santa Fe's institutional voice, the artist composed and recorded a number of songs/ press releases to publicize the exhibition. The songs deliver accurate information about the biennial, in the first person, through an unexpected combination of institutional promotional language, word play, and communication strategies ordinarily unavailable to the curators or administrators at SITE. In *Press Release Song #2*, a singer accompanied by a trombone bombastically lists the participating artists, but at each name mistakenly sings a word that rhymes with it.[8] He immediately corrects himself and pronounces the artist's name properly. This playful sequence repeats unfamiliar names and mispronunciations, signaling the Americas as a multilingual continent.

Navigating a foreign language with an accent— leaving sounds and traces of your mother tongue and its landscape around you—you involuntarily resist a structure from within. For the speaker, as for the siblings in the Cortázar story, there is acknowledgment that rooms have been taken over, though not yet the entire house. A structure of passive resistance infuses a structure of resistant acceptance.

In the video installation *Miraculous Fermentations*, 2018, Taylor further explores the connections among landscape, foreign accents, and legibility. The artist invited five German performers to read and sing a song in English that she composed with sentences originally written in German by Thomas Mann, or in English by LA–based writer and food critic Jonathan Gold. Representing a variety of regions in Germany, the performers bring distinct German accents to the lyrics. The video was shot in the Santa Monica Hills, in proximity to the house in Los Angeles where Mann lived in exile.

As soon as museum visitors, or guests, walk into the lobby of SITE Santa Fe, the host, they encounter two projects explicitly addressing museums and hospitality: a replica of the artist-run space NuMu (El Nuevo Museo de Arte Contemporáneo) and an installation by Andrea Fraser on the intersection of American museums and politics in the 2016 elections.

NuMu has been active since 2012, thanks to the vision and commitment of artists Stefan Benchoam and Jessica Kairé, who have created a space—the only one so far—dedicated to the support, exhibition, and documentation of contemporary art in Guatemala. Their exhibition program is housed in a small concrete structure (2 by 2.5 meters) originally designed as a drive-through egg-selling kiosk. Embracing the vernacular and the global, NuMu's exhibitions and projects support emerging, established, well-known, and forgotten artists and other figures from Guatemala and the rest of the world. In 2017, at the invitation of the Los Angeles County Museum of Art, a 1:1 replica of NuMu traveled from Guatemala to present three exhibitions within the museum (the work of Joaquín Orellana, Regina José Galindo, and the duo Donna Conlon/Jonathan Harker). *Casa tomada* will host the second stop of NuMu, which in turn will host *El nido salvage* (The wild nest), a project Radamés "Juni" Figueroa initiated in Guatemala in 2013, when he turned NuMu into a motel room (mirrors on the ceiling and all). Figueroa taps into the idea of the museum as a sheltered place for meaningful encounters, challenging its public vocation by turning it into a private, if hourly, space.

On the other side of the lobby, Fraser's project also questions the public calling of American museums by cross-referencing data to show the overlapping of museum patronage and contributions to the political campaigns leading to the election of Donald Trump as president of the US in 2016:

*Do private, nonprofit arts organizations funded and governed by wealthy patrons serve to legitimize government by and for the wealthiest members of society? Are the political activities and influence of the board members of arts organizations consistent with their trusteeship of our collective cultural heritage? These questions are not new, but they take on new urgency as the political influence of highly concentrated wealth in the United States increases, and as a growing number of politicians promote nationalism and intolerance to secure voter support for plutocratic governance, attacking the civil rights and liberties upon which depend not only the arts, but an open and democratic society.*[9]

Various forms of hosting and reciprocity have been at the center of Fernanda Laguna's work. During the last twenty years, she has been behind several dynamic and influential artist-run spaces in Buenos Aires, such as the legendary Belleza y Felicidad (1999–2008), and the less-known Tu Rito (2010–13), a gallery without doors and locks, where everything exhibited was susceptible to theft. Her extremely subjective and personal paintings represent a stark contrast with this public and social aspect of her work.

For *Casa tomada*, Laguna proposes a precarious paper structure emulating the section of a house, an amputated fragment that wandered off and now sits by itself in the gallery. A number of her own paintings—pictures inflicted by sentimentality, bad taste, disarming confidences, and a genuine urge to communicate —hang from the walls that she has decorated with wall-drawings depicting domestic paraphernalia. A painted house, as she calls it, presents a dysfunctional ghost house without mirrors, a place to run away from reflection.

The syndrome of the phantom limb—the
uncanny sensation that an amputated body
part is still attached, and on occasion even has
pains or itches—resonates deeply with the tales
of welcoming and eviction, hosts and ghosts,
briefly discussed in this essay. The phantom
house of *Casa tomada* evokes an amputation and
its replicas. In 1599, at the end of the sixteenth
century, the conquistador Juan de Oñate
ordered the amputation of the right feet of
twenty-four Acoma Pueblo prisoners. In 1997,
at the end of the twentieth century, the right
foot of the statue of Oñate in Alcalde, New
Mexico, went missing. The monument to the
"Last Conquistador" was defaced with surgical,
orthopedic precision. The statue was restored
soon thereafter, but that certainly didn't abate
the itch.

ENDNOTES

1.  Jacques Derrida, *Of Hospitality: Anne Dufourmantelle Invites Jacques Derrida to Respond*, trans. Rachel Bowlby (Stanford, CA: Stanford University Press, 2000), 17.

2.  After arriving in Patagonia in the sixteenth century, Spanish colonists hunted the Kawésqar like animals. In the nineteenth century, a group of eleven Kawésqar people were sent to appear in zoos and fairs in Berlin and Paris, and only four returned alive. Rodrigo Bustamente, "130 años después regresan los kawésqar," BBC online, Mundo, January 14, 2010, www.bbc.com/mundo/america_latina/2010/01/100114_1626_chile_indigenas_gtg.shtml.

3.  "At the beginning of [the twentieth] century, the State as a colonizing agent promoted the prospection and relocation of the austral ethnic groups, placing them in a terminal situation by the effects of their own actions. They were gathered in small groups and reduced to the sedentary lifestyle of the assistance agencies; that is, control of a forced reconversion." Justo Pastor Mellado, "The Nomadic Photography of Paz Errázuriz," in Paz Errázuriz, *Los Nómadas del Mar* (Santiago de Chile: Museo Nacional de Bellas Artes, 1996), unpaginated.

4.  In an interview held by the UNESCO in conjunction with the International Day of the World's Indigenous Peoples in 2013, Juan Carlos Tonko, leader of the Kawésqar people, discusses his people's demand for the restoration of rights to their ancestral lands. UNESCO website, August 2, 2013, http://www.unesco.org/new/en/media-services/single-view/news/juan_carlos_tonko_leader_of_the_kawesqar_people_my_peopl/.

5.  Mellado, "Nomadic Photography of Paz Errázuriz," n.p.

6.  "Photographs can create images but they are not images per se, they are things, a physical object. An image doesn't have to be based on a photograph. It is a mind-picture, or an image is a picture in the mind. A photograph may inspire or foment an image or images. An image is a concoction, often manufactured, meant to create a way to be seen, viewed, understood. It can be aerie faerie, a phantom, phantasm. Can an image built out of self-consciousness lie?" Lynne Tillman, *Men and Apparitions* (New York: Soft Skull Press, 2018), 6.

7.  The passage about the artists' role reads: "J: does that sound like a safari? / A: no, that's what the others do / J: what? / A: hunt exotic animals / J: what do we do then? / A: realize we're part of the beast / J: so what makes us different? / A: our appetite / J: and what makes us the same? / A: our appetite / J: how do we begin our ascent into the bowels of the beast? / A: more like a descent, a steep descent into its intestines. we're already in there anyway."

8.  Derrida again: "The right to hospitality commits a household, a line of descent, a family, a familial or ethnic group receiving a familial or ethnic group. Precisely because it is inscribed in a right, a custom, an ethos and a *Sittlichkeit*, this objective morality . . . presupposes the social and familial status of the contracting parties, that it is possible for them to be called by their names, to have names, to be subjects in law, to be questioned and liable, to have crimes imputed to them, to be held responsible, to be equipped with nameable identities, and proper names. A proper name is never purely individual." Derrida, *Of Hospitality*, 17.

9.  Andrea Fraser, "It's Time to Consider the Links Between Museum Boards and Political Money," artnet website, May 7, 2018, excerpted from her book *2016 in Museums, Money, and Politics* (Cambridge, MA: MIT Press, 2018), https://news.artnet.com/art-world/how-are-museums-implicated-in-todays-political-mess-1278824.

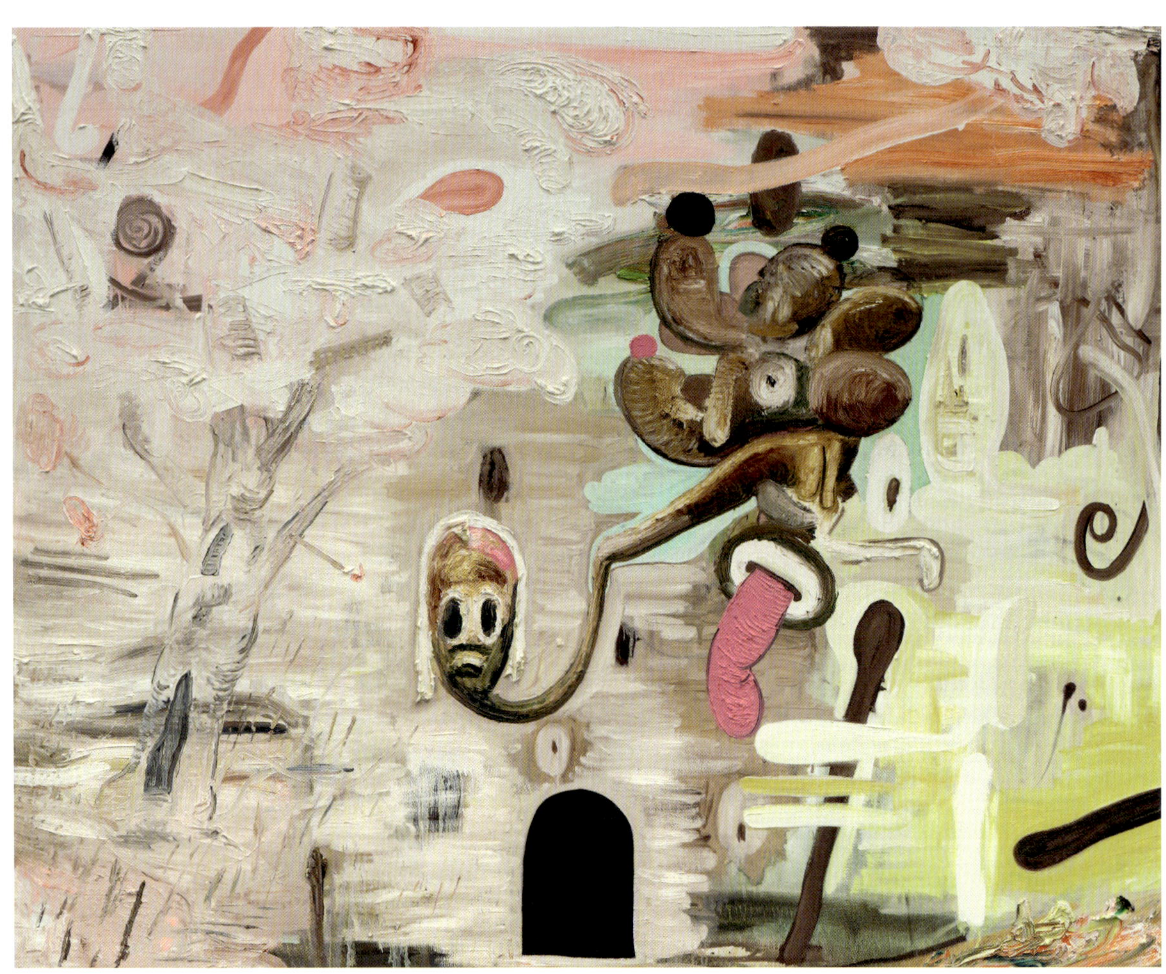

Victor Estrada, *The Spirit of the Living and the Dead and Cotton Candy / Posada*, 2017

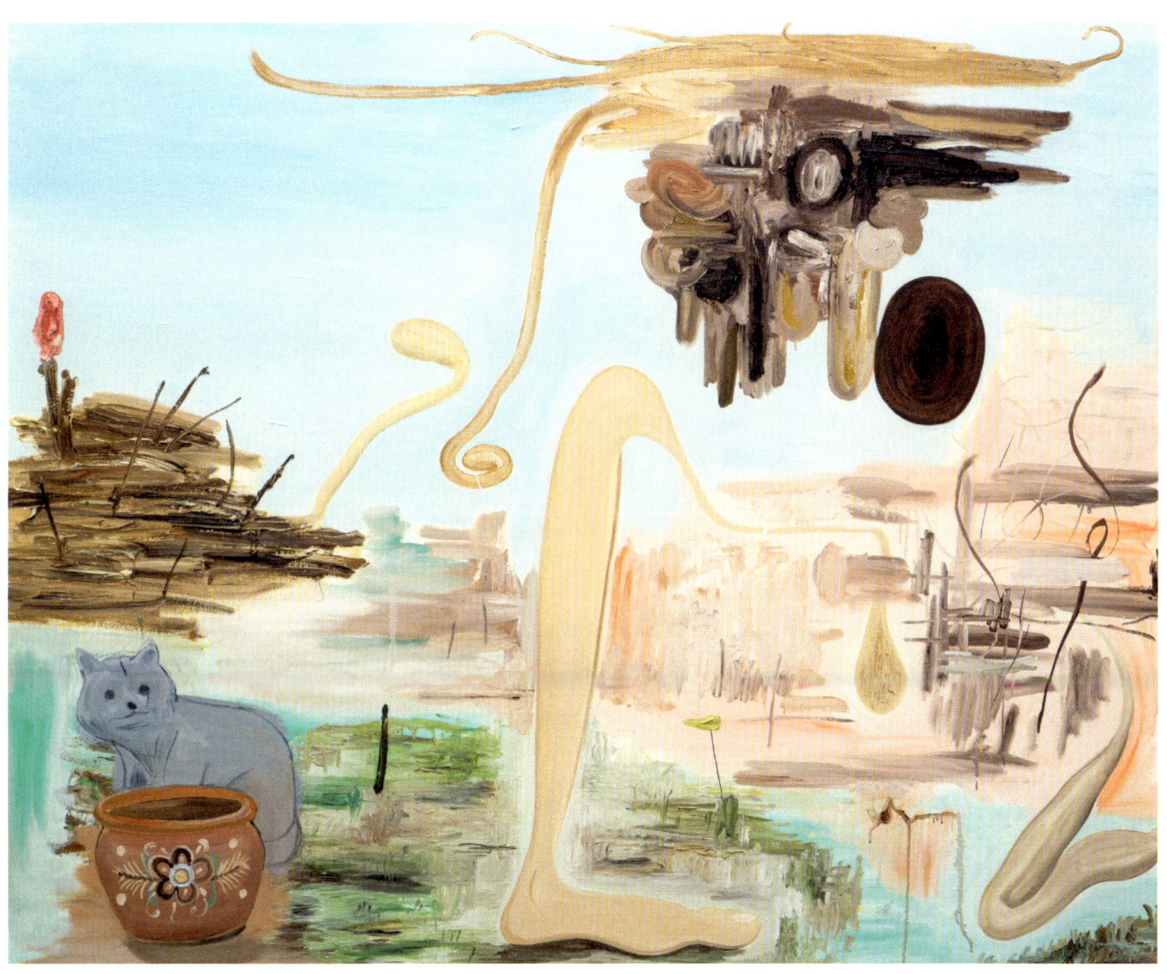

*I Went Walking and She Threw Me a Look / aka "Froggie Went a Courtin", 2017*

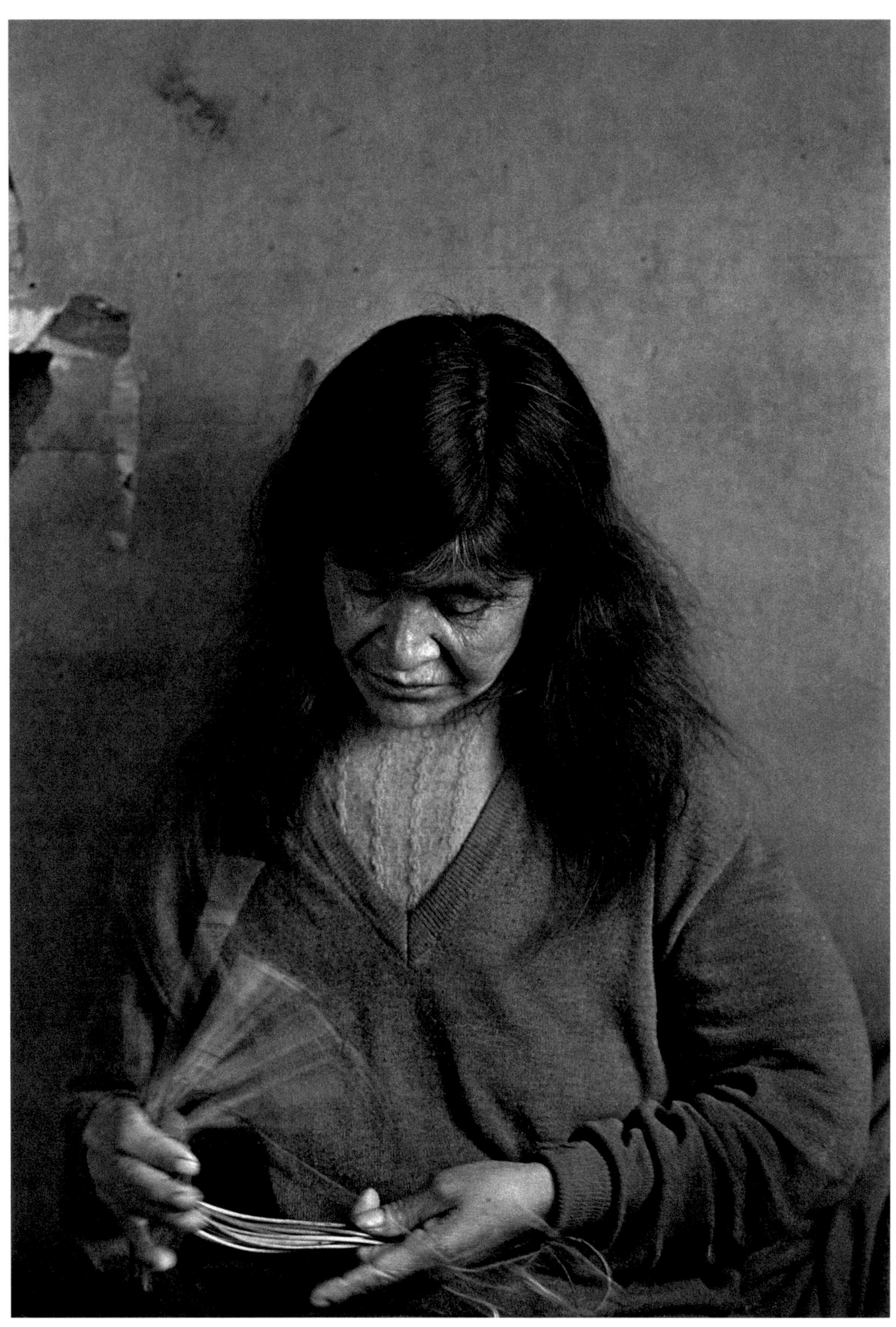

Paz Errázuriz, from the series *Nómadas del mar* (Nomads of the sea), 1996

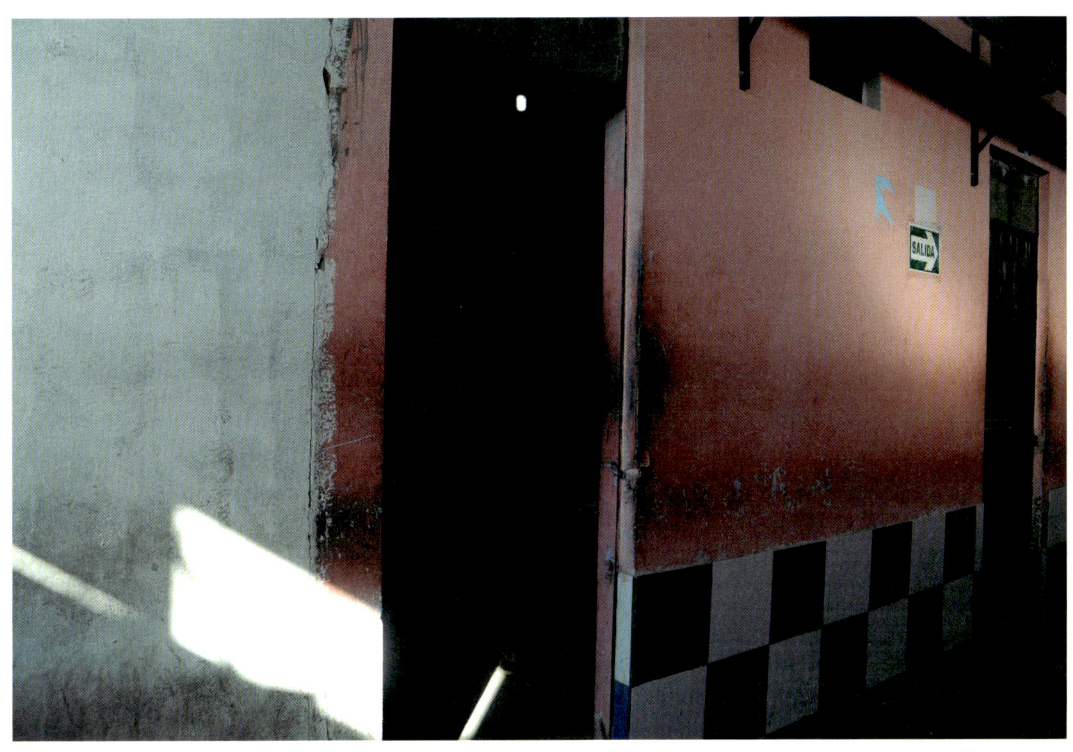

From the series *Niñas* (Girls), 2018
Made with contributions by Sergio Parra

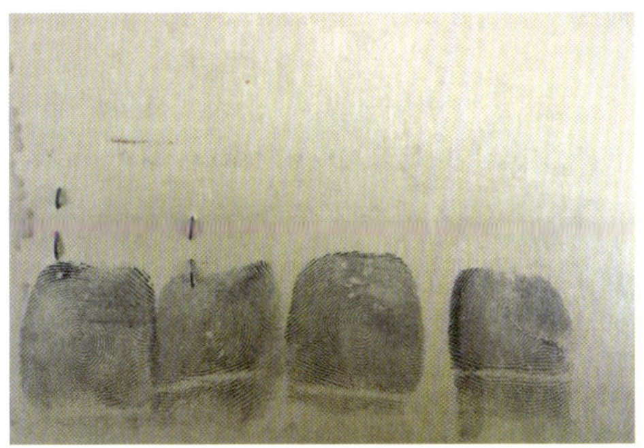

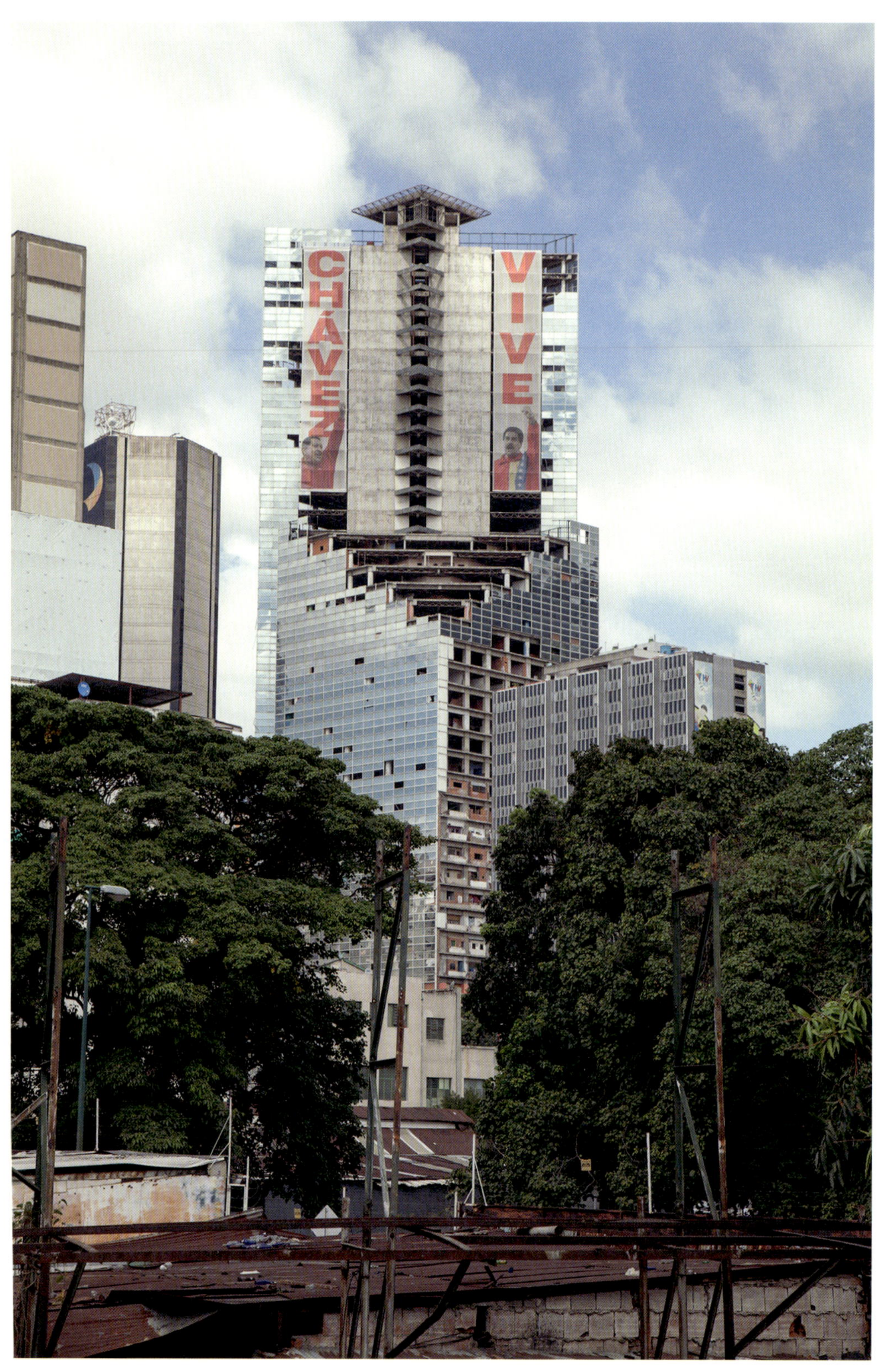


Ángela Bonadies and Juan José Olavarría, from *La Torre de David*, 2010–ongoing

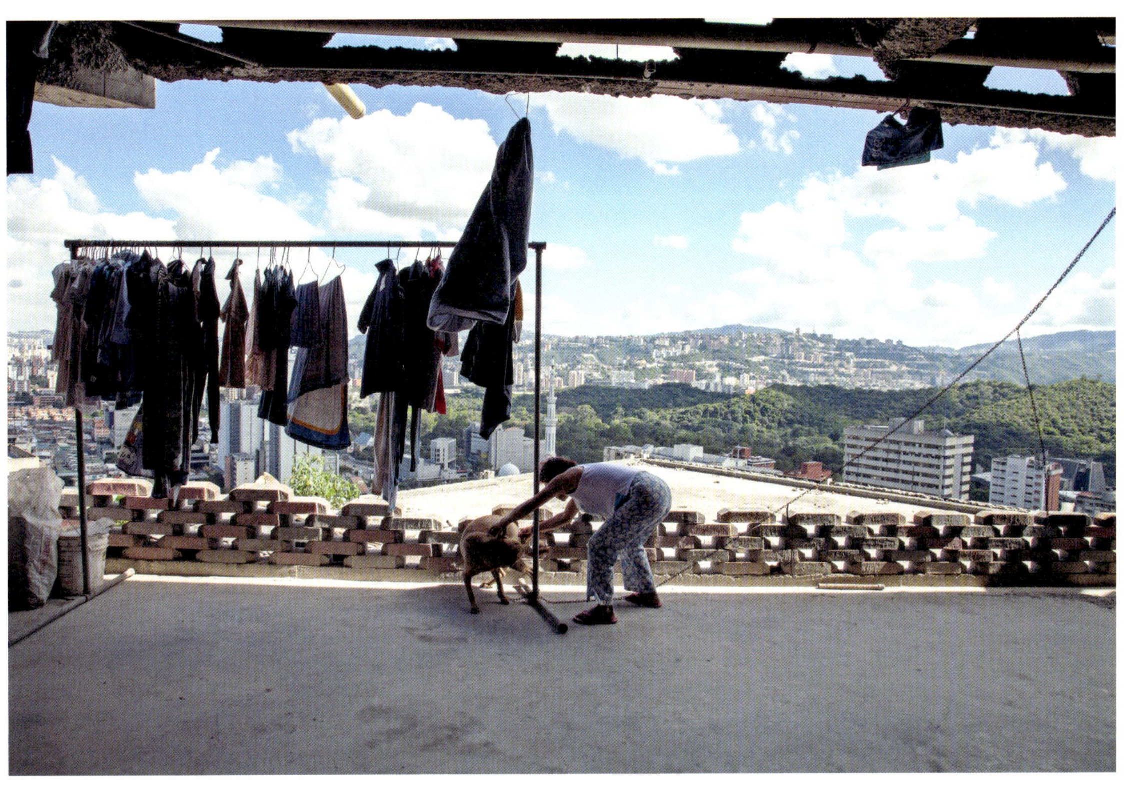

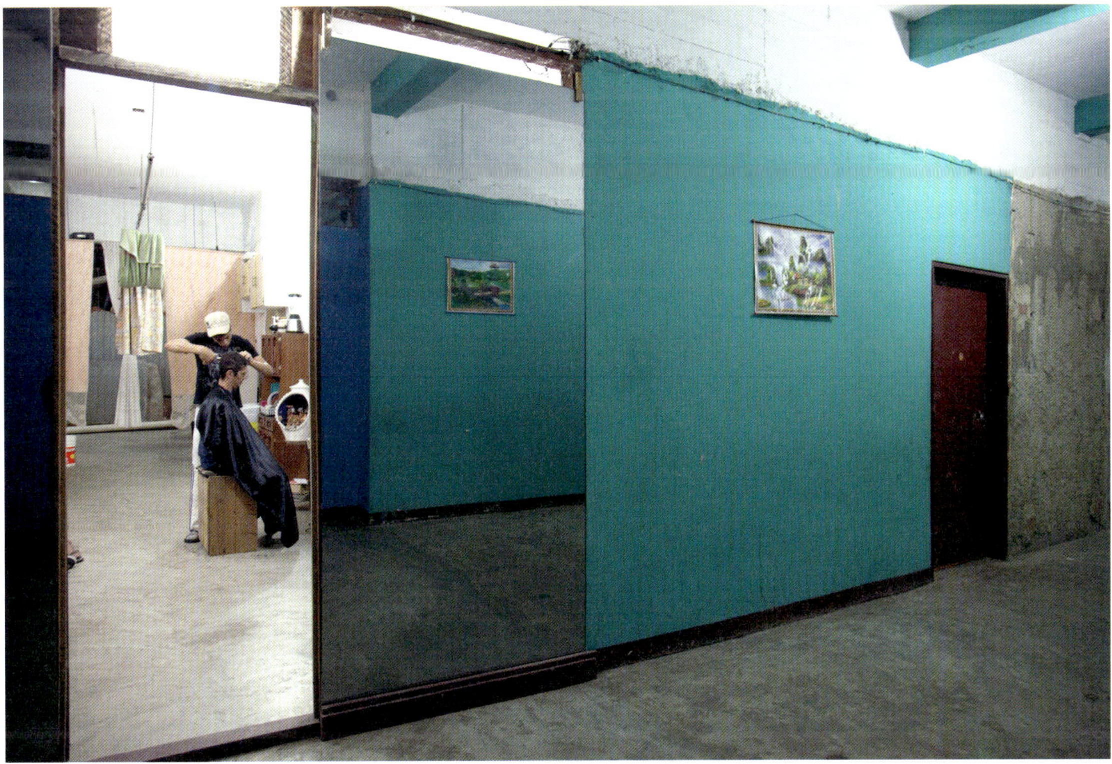

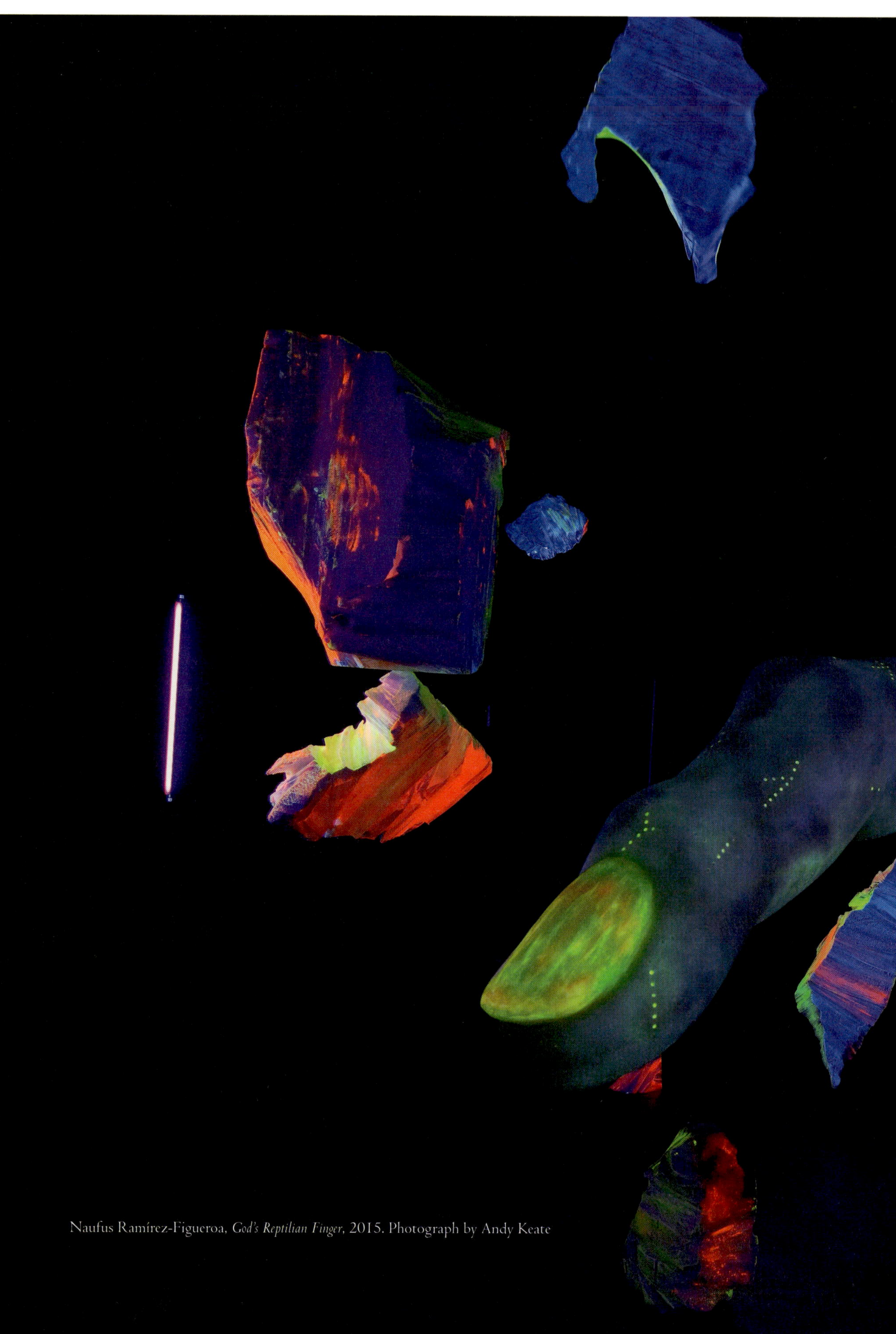

Naufus Ramírez-Figueroa, *God's Reptilian Finger*, 2015. Photograph by Andy Keate

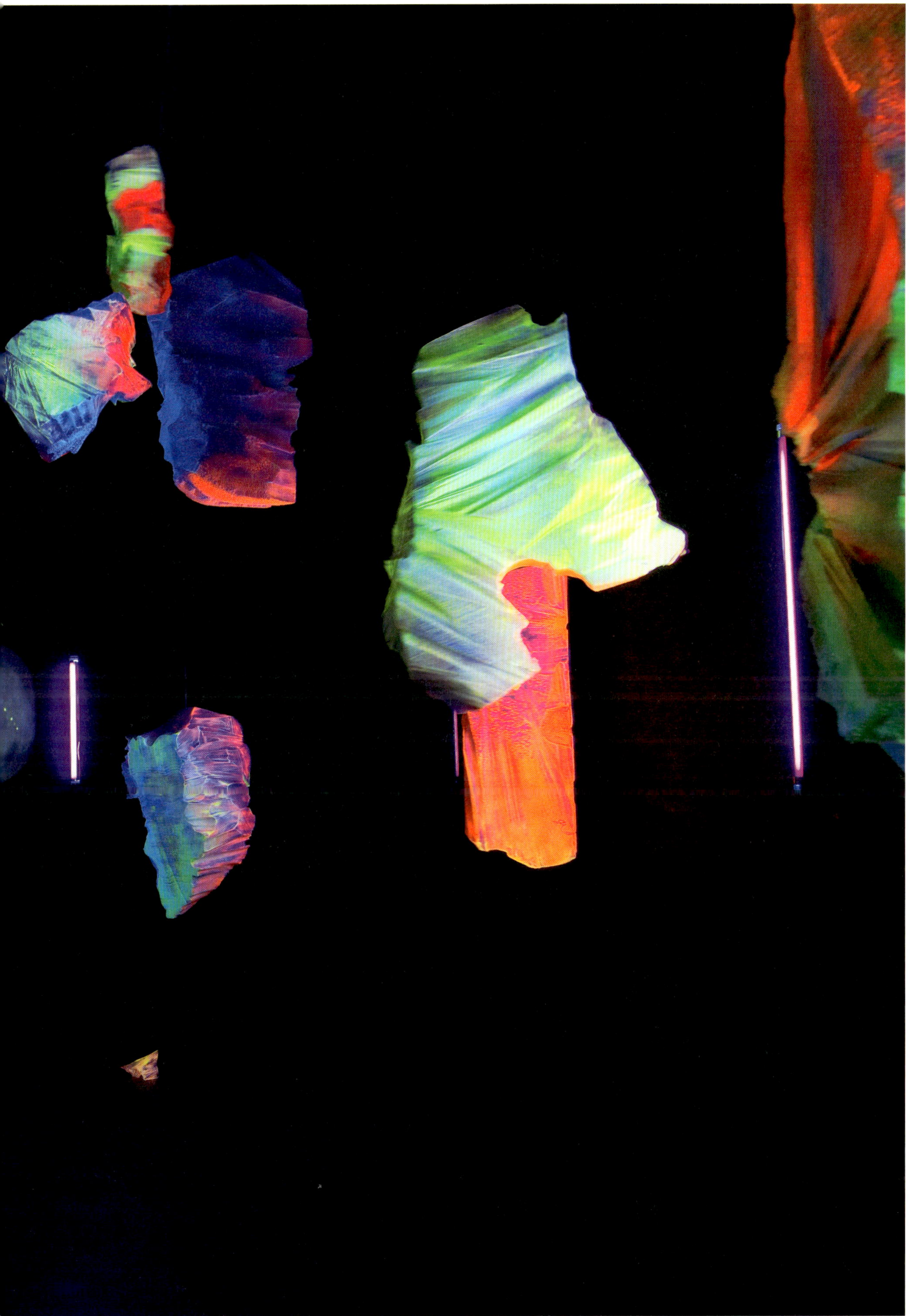

# Sitelines Press Release #2

Trombone/Voice

Stephanie Taylor
arr. Casey Butler

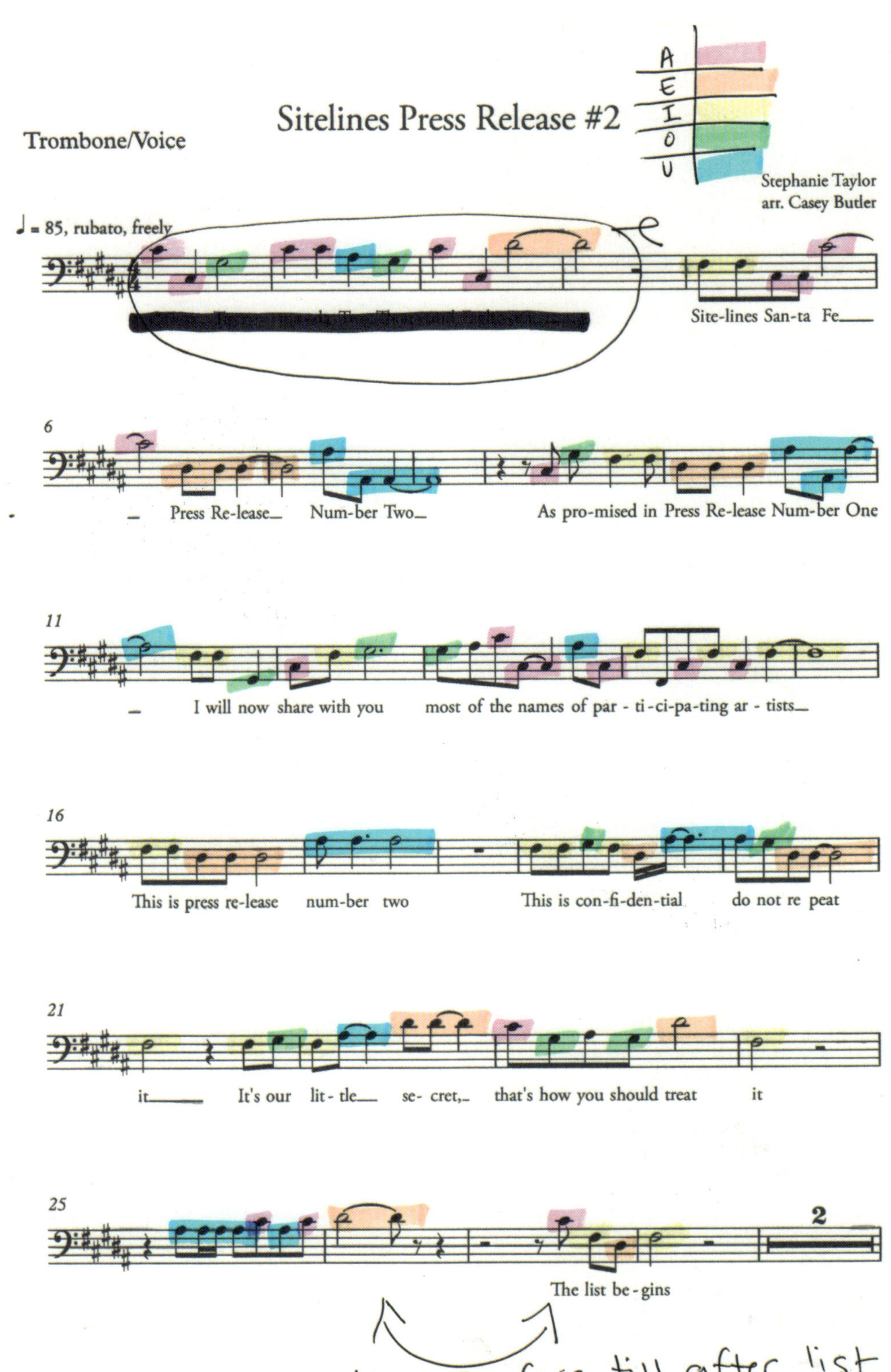

Trombone/Voice

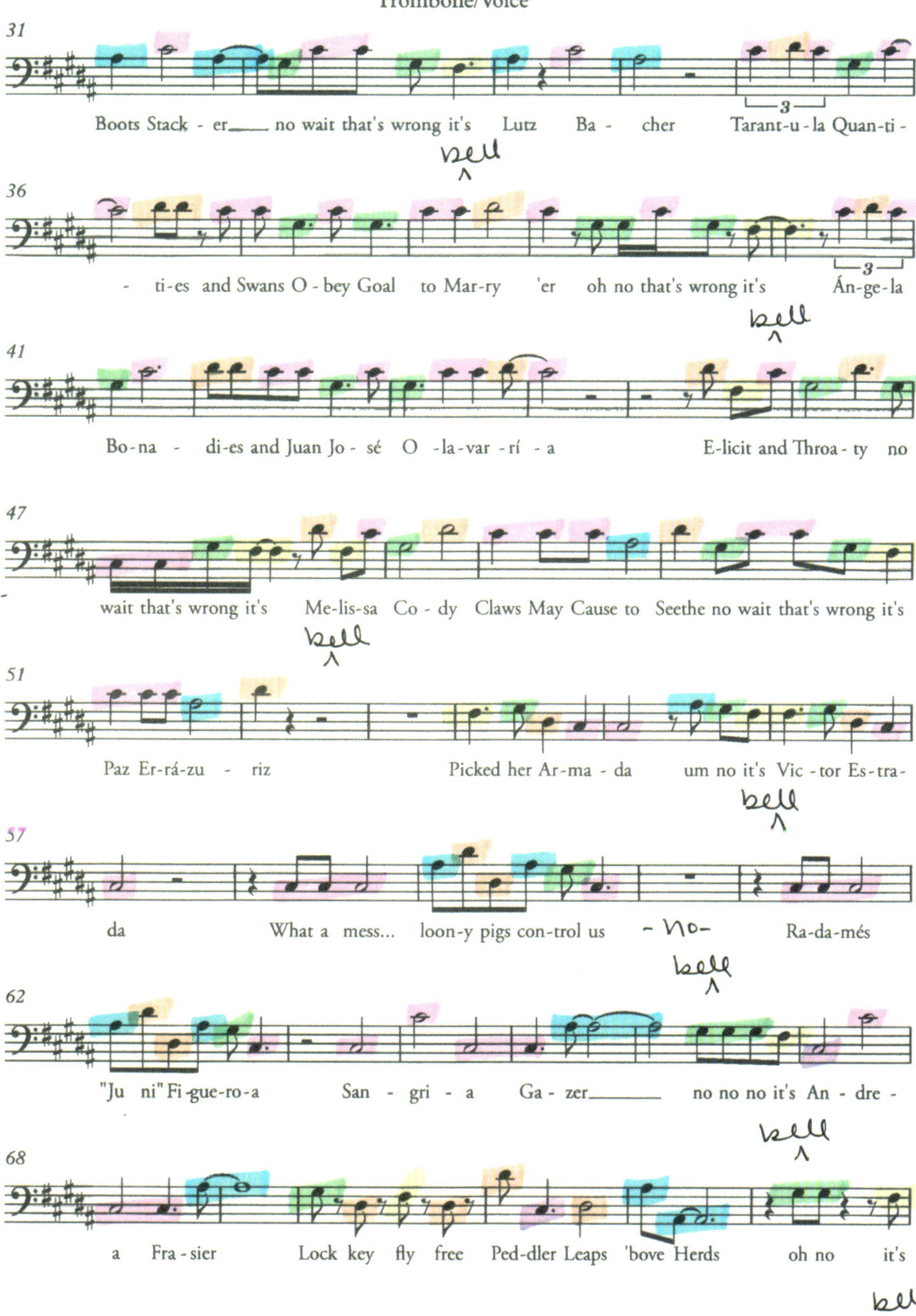

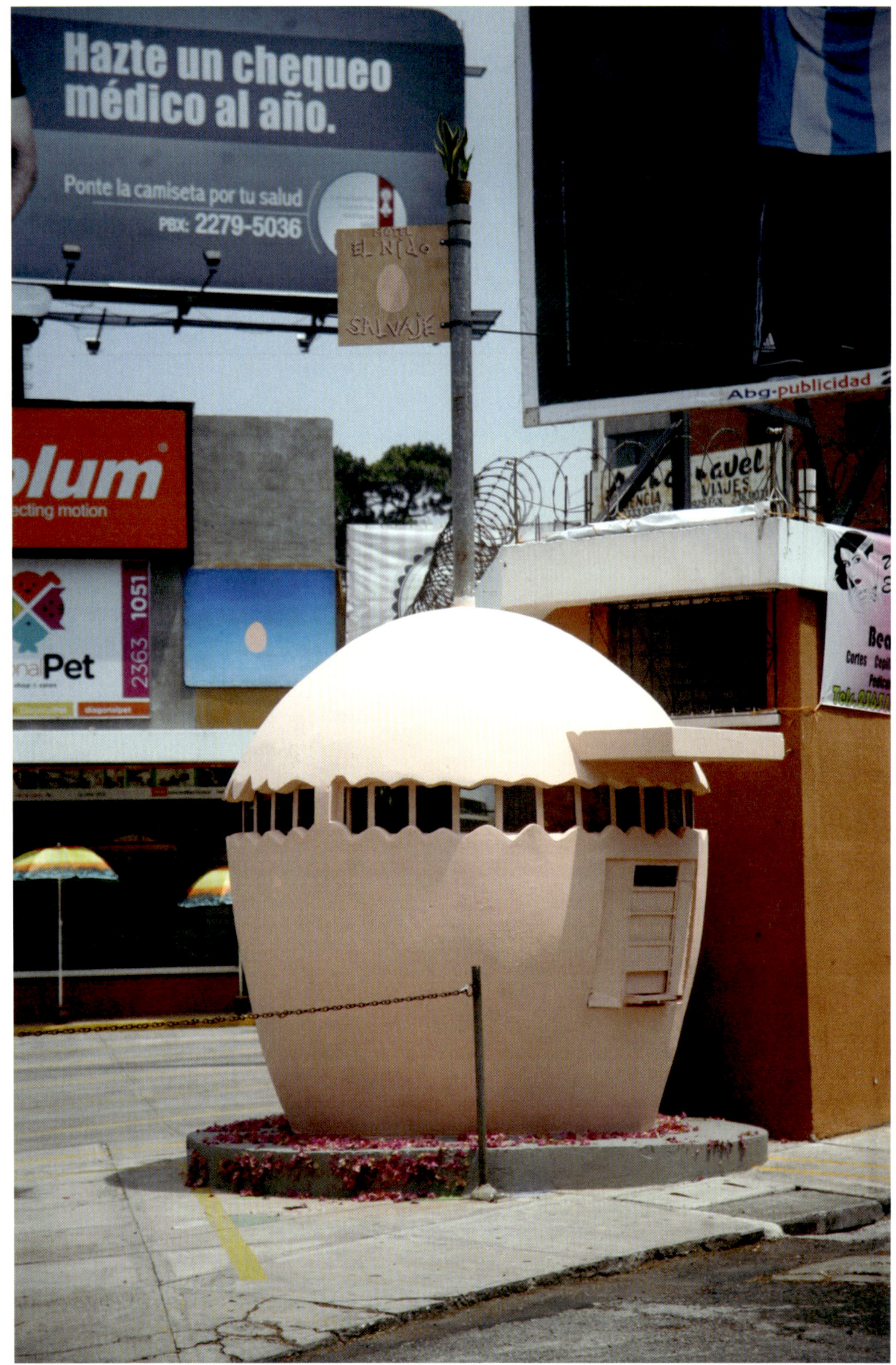

NuMu (El Nuevo Museo de Arte Contemporáneo), 2013

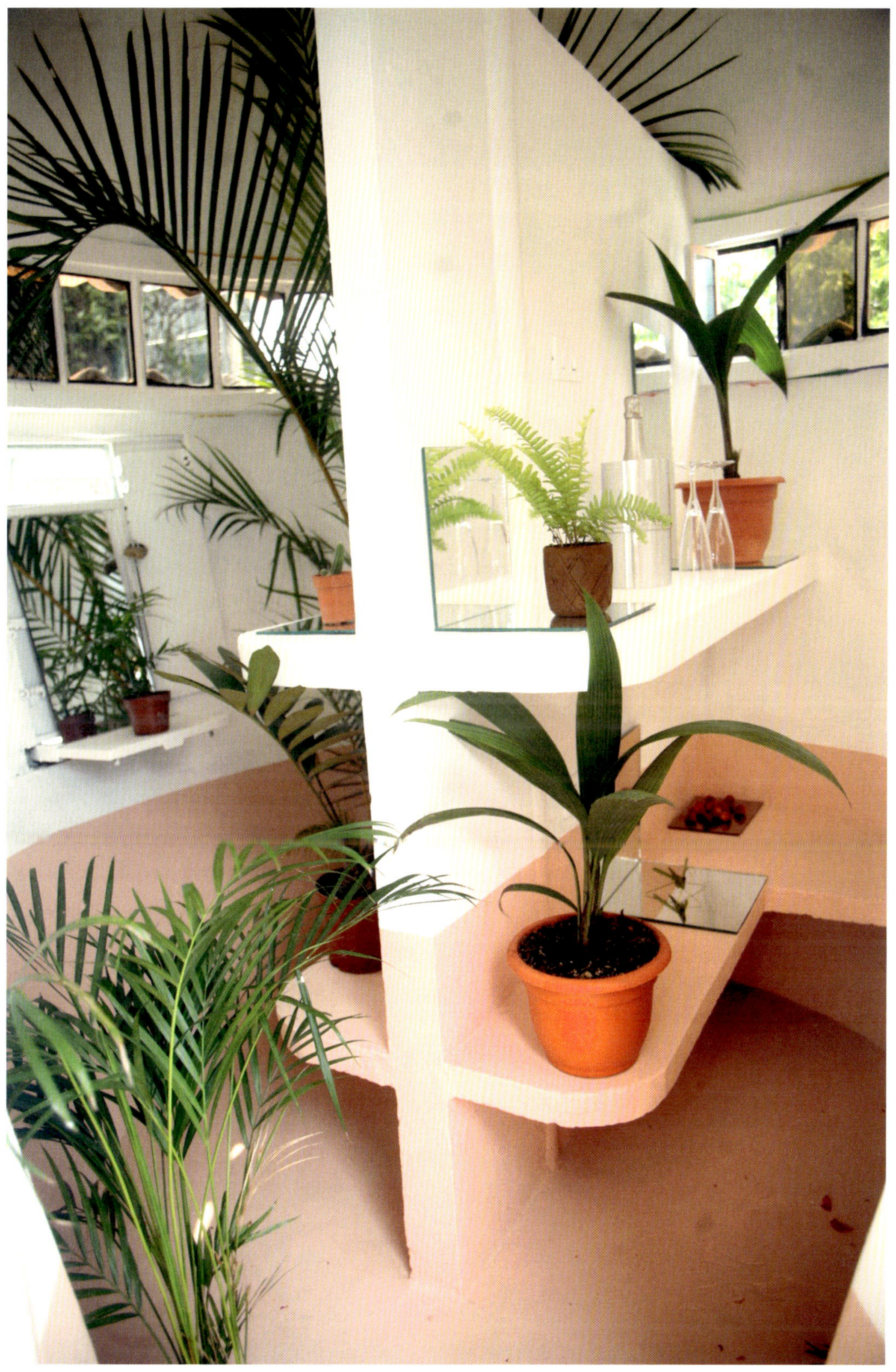

Radamés "Juni" Figueroa, *El nido salvaje* (The wild nest), 2013

## TOTAL CONTRIBUTIONS FOR ALL LIKELY POLITICAL CONTRIBUTION RECORDS FOUND BY PARTISAN OR IDEOLOGICAL ORIENTATION*

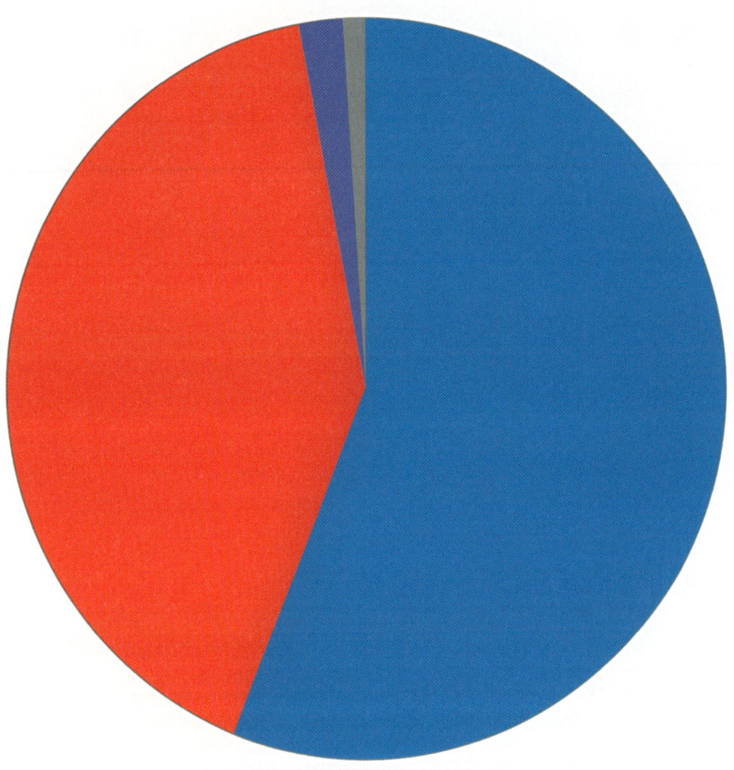

Total contributions for all likely records found: $212,405,878
Democratic/Liberal: $121,328,349 (57.1%)
Republican/Conservative: $89,218,587 (42%)
Both parties: $1,218,916 (0.6%)
Non-partisan, third-party, and unknown: $640,026 (0.3%)

*Contributions listed with board members are "likely" because identification could not be made with complete certainty in every case.

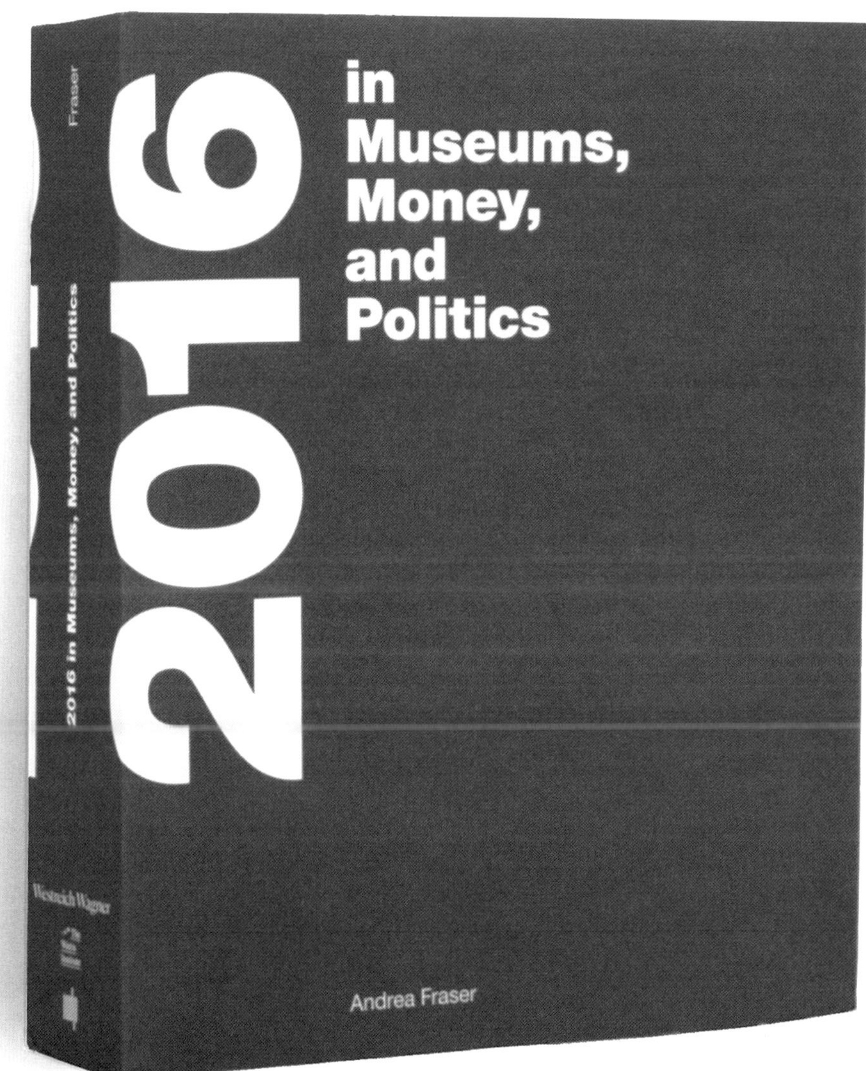

Andrea Fraser, *2016 in Museums, Money, and Politics*, 2018

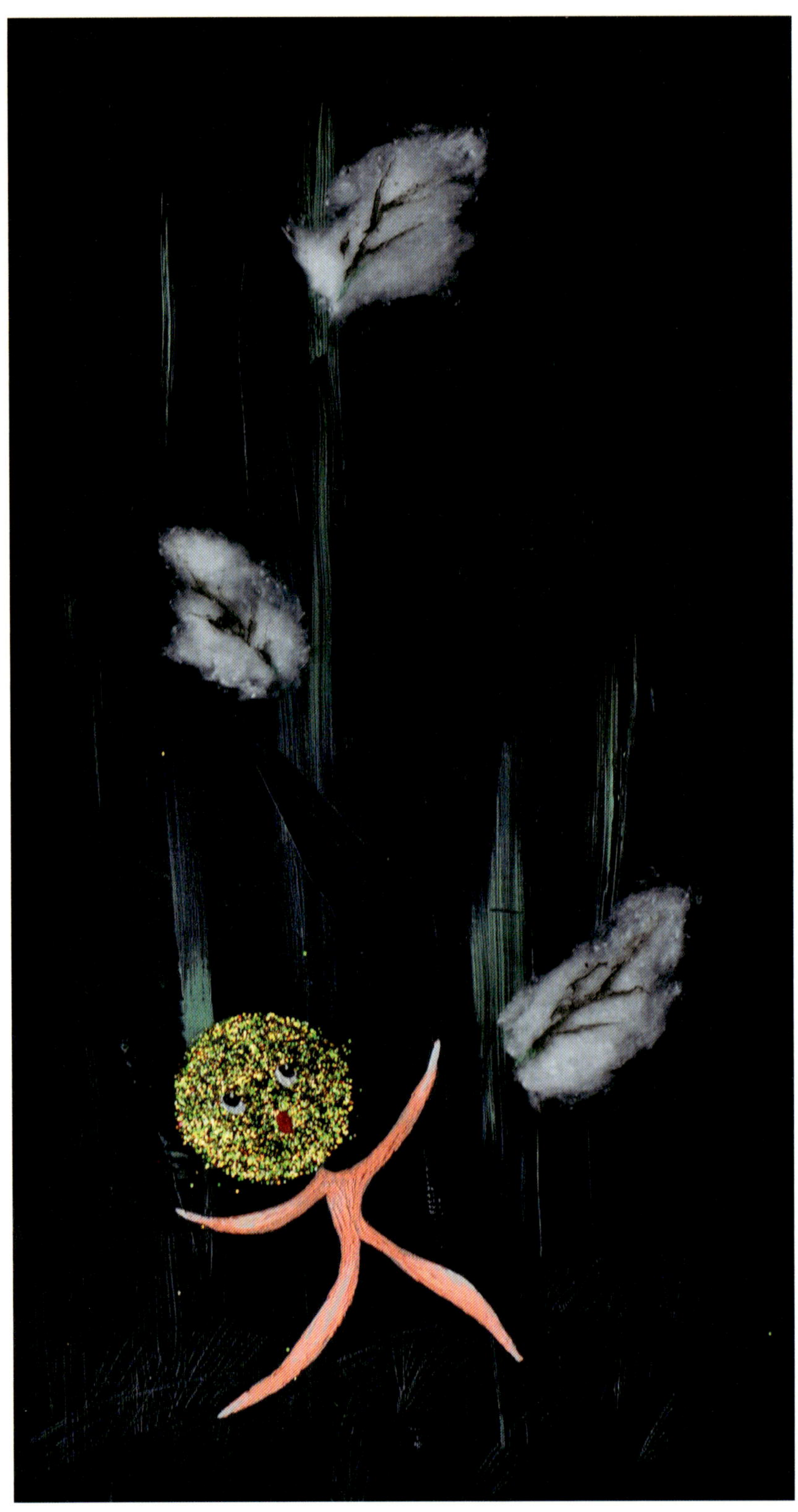

Fernanda Laguna, *Mi yo escondido II* (My hidden self II), 2017

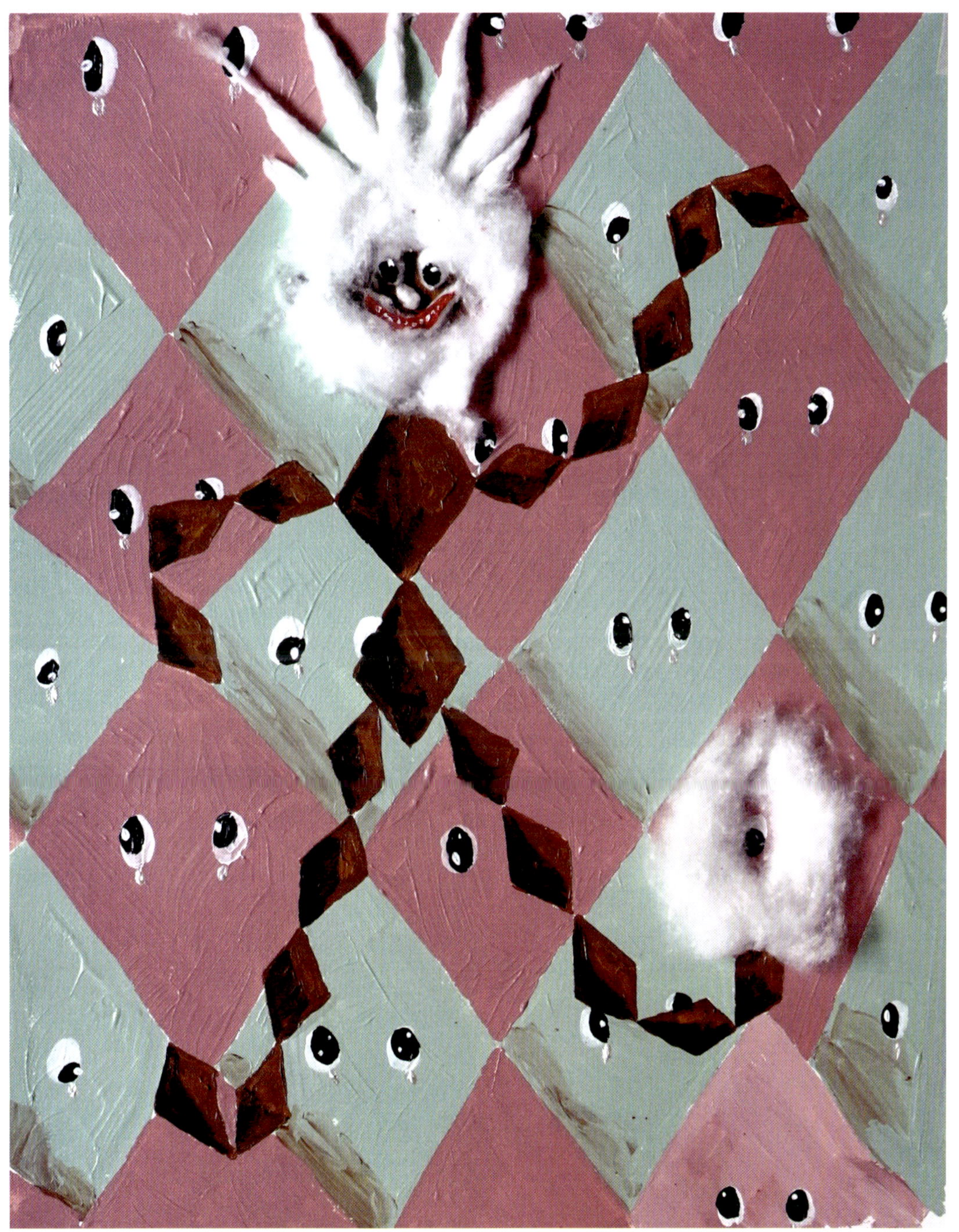

*Untitled*, 2017

# YOU MIGHT SAY THAT THE MASTERS NEVER SAW IT COMING

Candice Hopkins

At the moment, language is becoming fragmented, polarized, and increasingly essentialized. The voices of the extreme left and the extreme right are starting to speak in the same tongue, their statements and actions underpinned with anxieties of identity, rising nationalism, and fears of marginalization. *Casa tomada* co-curator José Luis Blondet relayed in an early meeting that it was when the right adopted the language of the left (and vice versa) that the political system in his home country of Venezuela broke down. When the middle ground erodes away, what comes to fill its space?

Anxieties about identity and the Other are once again taking political form. They are manifesting materially in things like the border wall prototypes presently installed near Otay Mesa, California. They are manifesting legally in travel bans from subjectively selected countries that inherently serve to further bias, injustice, and unrest. They are manifesting personally in the mutual suspiciousness of groups of people. Anxiety breeds mischaracterization, as when a police officer tries to justify the shooting of a Black man in the back by stating that he "feared for his life," or when a young white supremacist fears that his

"rights" are being threatened and guns down nine Black parishioners and children. More subtly, a woman called 911 on two prospective university students, Native Americans from New Mexico, for being "too quiet" and having strange emblems on their shirts, making her feel "creeped out." In her call, she described them as Hispanic and stated that one was "from Mexico."[1] This is civil society and civil rights deteriorating. This is the middle ground slipping away.

This deterioration has a particular rhetoric. As part of our curatorial research and conversations, we began to listen more closely to the words used to distinguish the authentic from the inauthentic, the narratives used to describe official and unofficial histories concerning who "belongs" and who does not. We also turned our attention to the instances when words fail, to the stutters, the mistakes, and the rise of neologisms—how the descriptor "the wall" rose to replace nuanced discussions on immigration, manufacturing hate while dangling an all-too-simple solution. The wall is a hardened manifestation of the divide between "us" and "them." But we also began to listen to other narratives, stories in which those described as lacking in power begin to turn the tables in order to restore the space of freedom—freedom of thought, freedom of imagination—a space where words have both power and play.

The sacred book of the K'iche' Maya people, *Popol Vuh*, contains an extraordinary moment. This moment doesn't concern the usual fears, like losing your land to outsiders (although at the time of the book's writing, the Spanish had already arrived to forcefully claim Indigenous lives and land through the manifest rights supposedly embodied by what they termed *encomienda*[2]). Nor is it a simple tale of "us versus them," a reductive opposition employed to great effect at present by both the right and the left. The moment I am speaking of is a peculiar rebellion. You might say that the masters never saw it coming. Words (and stories) for K'iche' people living in what is now Guatemala have the "ability to survive the death of [their] author," and thus embody the idea of *k'atajisaj*, meaning "to cause to have life."[3] K'iche' poetry is not based on rhyme or metrical rhythms, but rather the arrangement of concepts into innovative and even ornate parallel structures. In *Popul Vuh*, "seldom are the authors content with expressing a single idea without embellishing it with synonymous concepts, metaphors, or descriptive epithets."[4] Poetic justice is literally expressed in a scenario where things that are overlooked—everyday kitchen utensils, including maize grinders and cooking griddles—rebel against those who wield them:

> *Then spoke also their griddles and their pots to them: "Pain you have caused us. Our mouths and our faces are sooty. You were forever throwing us upon the fire and burning us. Although we felt no pain, you now shall try it. We shall burn you," said all of their pots. Thus their faces were all crushed. The stones of the hearth flattened them. They would come out from the fire, landing on their heads and causing them pain. They fled. They hurried away. They wanted to climb up on top of the houses, but the houses would fall apart beneath them and they were thrown off.[5]*

English is ill-equipped to provide a sense of the conceptual complexity of the Mayan original without extensive footnotes denoting the word play even in a single line. Yet the rebellion taking place in the lines above is still clear, the hierarchies of power radically shifted. As in Julio Cortázar's short story "Casa tomada," even the houses reject their owners. For Naufus Ramírez-Figueroa, this is an apt metaphor for the aftermath of the Guatemalan Civil War, when the Mestiza/o community started to gain a semblance of power in Guatemalan society, complicating centuries of Spanish colonial rule.

Over the course of her career, Victoria Mamnguqsualuk, born in a traditional encampment near Garry Lake in what is now Nunavut, often returned to the same character, Kiviuq (alternatively spelled Qiviuq, Keeveok, or Kivioq, and, in Greenland, Qooqa). A migrant, he travels through different lands as well as through different times and different cultures. He is one of the oldest figures in Inuit oral tradition. and his stories likely go back thousands of years. He resurfaces at significant moments—he is known to have intercepted a Soviet satellite flying over the Arctic during the Cold War (during this period the Canadian Arctic was the front line, and Inuit first-hand witnesses), and after many lives passed in the world of the white man, he finally returned home to forewarn of what he saw while away.

The real and the imaginary generatively rub up against each other in these stories, in ways that have often confused their interpretation by outsiders. For Inuit, people and spirits commonly "share the same natural environment."[6] Mamnguqsualuk's prints, drawings, and textiles are no exception. We see humans convening with snake spirits (in one print, a person emerges from the body of a hulking yellow serpent); fish are monstrously large; and people are often in a state of transformation, sometimes mutating into seals or birds, while animals in turn become human. Importantly, "all that is described in [these stories] really did happen once, when everything in the world was different to what it is now."[7] Artists often work in the in-between, in the space of invention (including the invention of the Other and of ourselves). In the in-between there is room for interplay between the assumed boundaries of human and animal, between what is true and what is made up. This is a generative space to inhabit. In this liminal realm our current preoccupation with fixed definitions and fixed symbols (think of the ominous return of the Confederate flag) begins to fray.

Jamasee (formerly transcribed as Jamasie) Pitseolak is also from the Arctic. Unlike Mamnguqsualuk, he is from a generation born in settlements. (In the 1960s, the scarcity of food resulting from an ecological collapse brought about by the fur trade forced Mamnguqsualuk's family to relocate permanently to Baker Lake, in what is now Nunavut. Before then, like many others, they lived a customary semi-nomadic lifestyle.) Early in Pitseolak's practice, he collected small bits of scrap stone—discarded and broken pieces as well as those considered inadequate for carving. From these he made intricate sculptures that, while carved, cannot exactly be called carvings. They are, more accurately, "additive sculptures."[8] Along with printmaking, carving is the dominant artistic medium in the North. The technique gives Pitseolak a great deal of room for material invention—in his sculpture of a tiny sewing machine there are many moving parts; the finely carved handle turns on a small stone axle, and when the wheel is rotated, it looks as though the needle might move up and down.

Pitseolak's material manifestations take on a character all their own. Many of his stone and antler sculptures entail word play: in *Toe Nailed*, 2006, a nail made of antler is drilled through a realistic stone toenail; in another, *Laden Sole*, 2004, an intricately detailed boot is chained to a heavy weight. Despite the humor, the spiritual and material transformations that characterize much Inuit art also have a place in Pitseolak's works. Unlike in the past, these transformations are not between people and animals, but between animals and other things. *Musk Ox Pistol*, 2011, is just what it says it is, a pistol with a musk ox in place of a handle, animating the entire sculpture. The barrel of the gun strapped to the animal's back is a heavy burden to carry, especially now.

There is a strand in Melissa Cody's practice that is likewise centered on words and phrases.

In her deft hands, woven text forms tactile poems, as in *US*, 2015:

US

LUST

OUSR

VUSU

EUSS

DUST

US

*Lust* turns to *dust*, and pressed between the vertical *loved* (in the past tense) and *trust* is the bond implied by *us*. Other weavings speak of "indelible memories" and "invisible tears." These feel personal, emanating a productive affect that is carefully crafted. They embed yet another loss.

In a recent interview, Cody explains the source of Navajo Germantown weaving, a style that she uses in many of her own works. On the forced march of Diné people from their traditional territories bordered by four sacred mountains, known as the Long Walk, they made use of their limited rations to make new weavings. In Cody's words: "Within those rations were blankets made with wool that had been made in Germantown, Pennsylvania. So what they did was the weavers unraveled them and then rewove them into their own designs."[9]

The fifty-three marches that took place between 1864 and 1866 were a failed attempt at ethnic cleansing by the US Army. Soldiers torched homes, livestock, and crops to force people out. When the survivors reached the fenced-in piece of desert they called Hwéeldi—and the Army called Fort Sumner—many soon died from the dirty water and lack of food. (Others had already been shot or left to perish for slowing the caravans, including heavily pregnant women and elders.) Only when the Army realized the scale of the crisis in the camp and its inability to sustain human life did they recognize the gravity of the atrocity and let people return home. While the Long Walk is a defining moment in contemporary Diné identity, Cody's works move back and forth in time. She describes herself as a child of the video-game era, coming of age in the 1980s. Sections of certain of her weavings look like television static, produced when wires are crossed, the signal is lost, and everything turns black and white.

For Eric-Paul Riege, a hogan with looms in place of walls is the ancient home of Na'ashjé'íí Asdzáá (Spiderwoman). It is a sacred space, one of sanctuary, and a beginning, a womb. In a prior world, it was Na'ashjé'íí Asdzáá who taught Diné people to weave. To this day she lives atop a rock pinnacle in Canyon de Chelly. At various times, this home/sanctuary/woven womb is activated by performances by Riege. "I will be performing as a weaving," he states. "I embody the motions, gestures, and poses of the processes and histories that go into weaving."[10] A home, Riege notes, necessarily exists externally and internally, physically and figuratively. The actions around the home, what he calls "dance," enable him to inhabit different forms and materials, and to enact ideological transgressions. Much like the shapeshifting stories told in Mamnguqsualuk's drawings, prints, and textiles, dance is a means for Riege to *become* animal. Yet in his performances he embodies not only animals but also forms in flux, including "nature creating rituals of prayer and stories for healing, wellbeing."[11]

This idea of ritual and healing also informs the paintings and sculptures of Lawrence Paul Yuxweluptun. In *Floor Opener*, 2013, six figures gather around a stylized Northwest Coast ovoid on the floor. Some hold drums, others have their mouths open as if singing. A few look as though they are mid-dance. Some of their bodies are rendered solid, while others appear carved, with legs and feet inscribed with other faces, other beings. Dark wooden walls and large ceiling beams surround the figures; in the background, a door is open to the outside, where a single cloud hovers in the night sky. Yuxweluptun has painted many a ceremony in the sacred big house. It is as though he lifts the thin veil dividing the human-world and the spirit-world to provide them access to each other. Resting on a platform extending in front of the painting, a collection of brightly painted wooden ovoids resemble totemic trees. While many of Yuxweluptun's paintings are searing critiques of environmental destruction and the damaging effects of the capitalist system, examples like this instead create space for the representation of other belief systems. At the same time, they call on us to pay better attention and to take better care of all things in our midst. How can we make space for the voices sounding at the margins? How do we amplify the voices of dissent?

As winter turned to spring, we visited Hock E Aye Vi Edgar Heap of Birds at the studio of Michael McCabe, master printer at Fourth Dimension, with whom the artist was beginning a new monoprint series. This was fresh on the heels of the horrific gun violence unleashed at Parkland High School in Florida that killed seventeen and wounded seventeen more. It was the response of Parkland students that finally broke through language thick with political moralism. ("Pray for the victims" was a common response of politicians and lawmakers, including the sitting president).

On that visit, one print in particular stood out. The following words appeared on a crimson background: "Stop Active Shooter Cadet Autie Custer."[12] They bear repeating. These are words steeped in violence, words rescued from the amnesia of history. In response to the mainstream coverage of the now epidemic number of mass shootings in the US, many were pointing out that these assaults don't come out of nowhere. Less than a hundred years ago, the US military orchestrated the slaughter of hundreds of Native American children, women, and men in massacres across the country. These incidents recurred from north to south; some, like the killings at Wounded Knee, are familiar; others, like the Washita Massacre near present-day Cheyenne, Oklahoma, less so. In Heap of Bird's prints, George Custer is framed not as a hero but as an "active shooter." For the many Cheyenne and their allies who died November 26, 1868, this is who he was.

The words on other prints have a rhythm: "Navajo Don't You Know Love You So" or "Can of Coors Hey Ya Aye Yo." These song lyrics, from bands like The Police and various Native groups, are installed alongside words drawn from historical encounters. Others seek to reframe these encounters in the present: "Indian Still Target Obama Bin Laden Geronimo." Bias is embedded in language that takes aim at other targets.

But what about the times when words fail, when silence takes over? During the NoDAPL protests against the Dakota Access Pipeline, water protectors staged a powerful action. With elders leading, more than one thousand women walked to the bridge over what is now called the Missouri River to occupy the only middle ground between themselves and the police and private security firms called in to "protect" the interests of the corporations involved. When they reached the center of the bridge, the women stood together in absolute silence. As John Cage's composition *4′33″* (4 minutes and 33 seconds) revealed so long ago, silence is never truly silence. Soon, other sounds were amplified for those who had gathered—the sounds of terror and surveillance. Everyone present could hear the constant hum of drones overhead recording every move, the buzz of the private security firm's handheld radios, and the metallic clicks of police as they readied their guns and prepared canisters of tear gas.[13] The authorities were prepared for the usual forms of protest, but not for this one. In the absence of words, the women became another kind of critic, their silence a powerful affront to corporate abuse of power and the inability to think beyond the insatiable need for resources. The women's decision *not* to raise their voices, but to rely on their irreducible presence instead, became a destabilizing force.

Like those fearless women, art has a transfiguring capacity that allows us to hear in moments of silence, to open our ears rather than to close them.

ENDNOTES

1.  Quoted in Dakin Andone and Hollie Silverman, "A mom on a college tour called the cops on two Native American teens because they made her 'nervous,'" CNN online, https://edition.cnn.com/2018/05/04/us/colorado-state-university-racial-profiling-trnd/index.html.

2.  *Encomienda* is a Spanish term that came to signify "an institution whereby the Crown authorized Spaniards who participated in the Conquest to collect tribute and demand labor from the Indians in return for services such as military duty and providing for the *spiritual welfare* of Indians under their control" (emphasis added). *Popol Vuh: Sacred Book of the Quiché Maya People* (2003), trans. and ed. Allen J. Christenson, Mesoweb website, 2007, www.mesoweb.com/publications/Christenson/PopolVuh.pdf. The contradiction, of course, is that the Spanish provided little in the way of protection (their very arrival laid the path for the death of nearly 80 percent of Indigenous populations) or the "spiritual welfare" of Indigenous peoples, whom they forced into adherence of Christianity, violently subjugating local belief systems and knowledge that had been honed over thousands of years and were central to the health and spiritual well-being of the people in lands foreign to the Spanish.

3.  Ibid., 7.

4.  Ibid., 33.

5.  Ibid., 77.

6.  Charles Moore, foreword to Charles Moore, Victoria Mamnguqsualuk, and K. J. Butler, *Keeveeok, Awake!: Mamnguqsualuk and the Rebirth of Legend at Baker Lake* (Edmonton, CAN: University of Alberta, 1986), 8.

7.  Knud Rasmussen, *The Netsilik Eskimos: Social Life and Spiritual Culture* (Copenhagen, DNK: Gylendanske Boghandel, 1931), 207.

8.  This distinction in Pitseolak's practice was first brought to the author's attention in 2012 by Christine Lalonde, Associate Curator, Indigenous Art, National Gallery of Canada, Ottawa.

9.  Melissa Cody, quoted in "Navajo Textile Artist Melissa Cody Forges Her Own Path," *San Diego City Beat* online, March 20, 2018, http://sdcitybeat.com/culture/features/navajo-textile-artist-melissa-cody-forges-her-own-path/.

10.  Eric-Paul Riege, revised proposal for *SITElines.2018: Casa tomada*, portable document format (PDF) file.

11.  Ibid.

12.  "Cadet Auster Custer" was used to refer to George Custer during the massacre at Washita Creek, "Cadet" alluding to his military beginnings, and "Autie" to his early nickname.

13.  This account of the sounds of Standing Rock was relayed to me by the composer Raven Chacon, who spent almost two weeks in the encampment. During that time, he recorded much of what he heard, including the women's "silent" protest on the bridge.

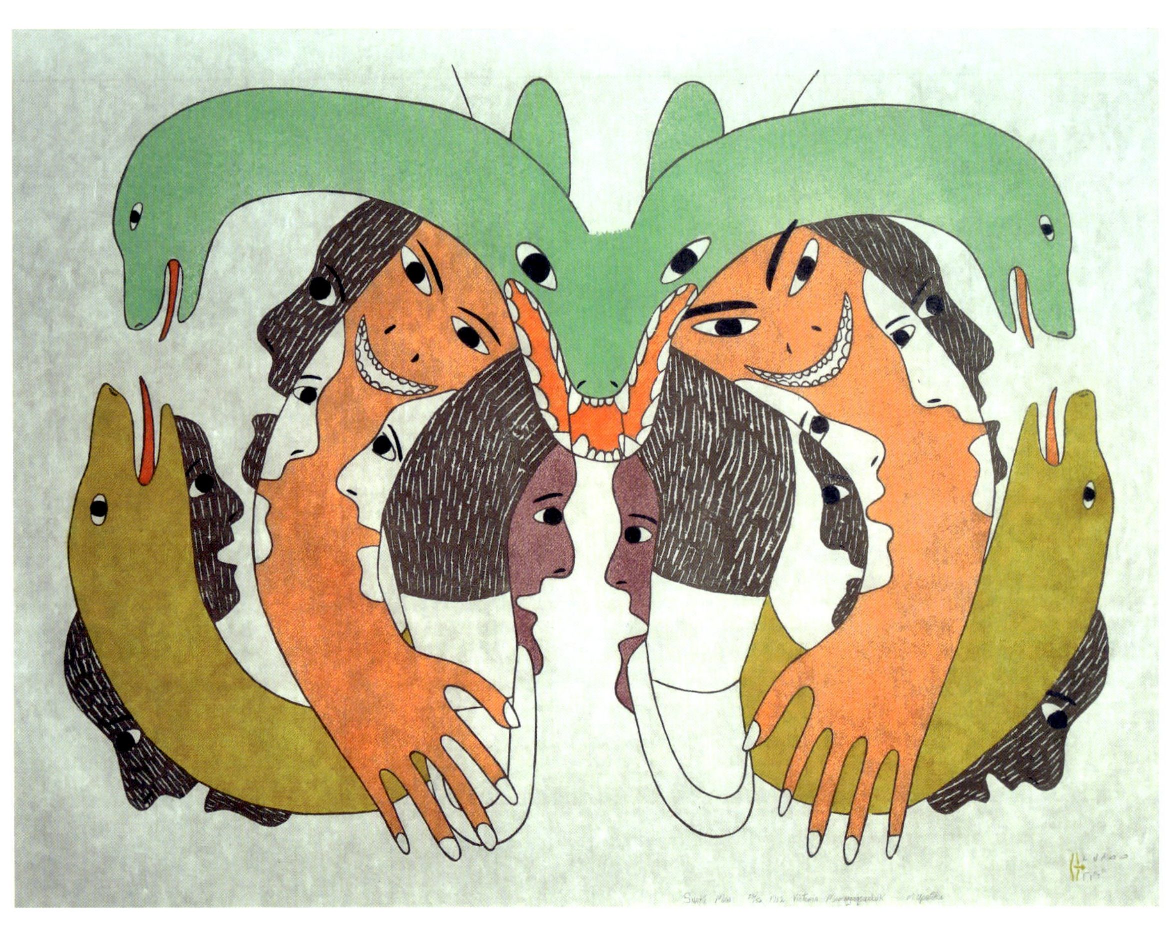

Victoria Mamnguqsualuk, *Snake Man*, 1982

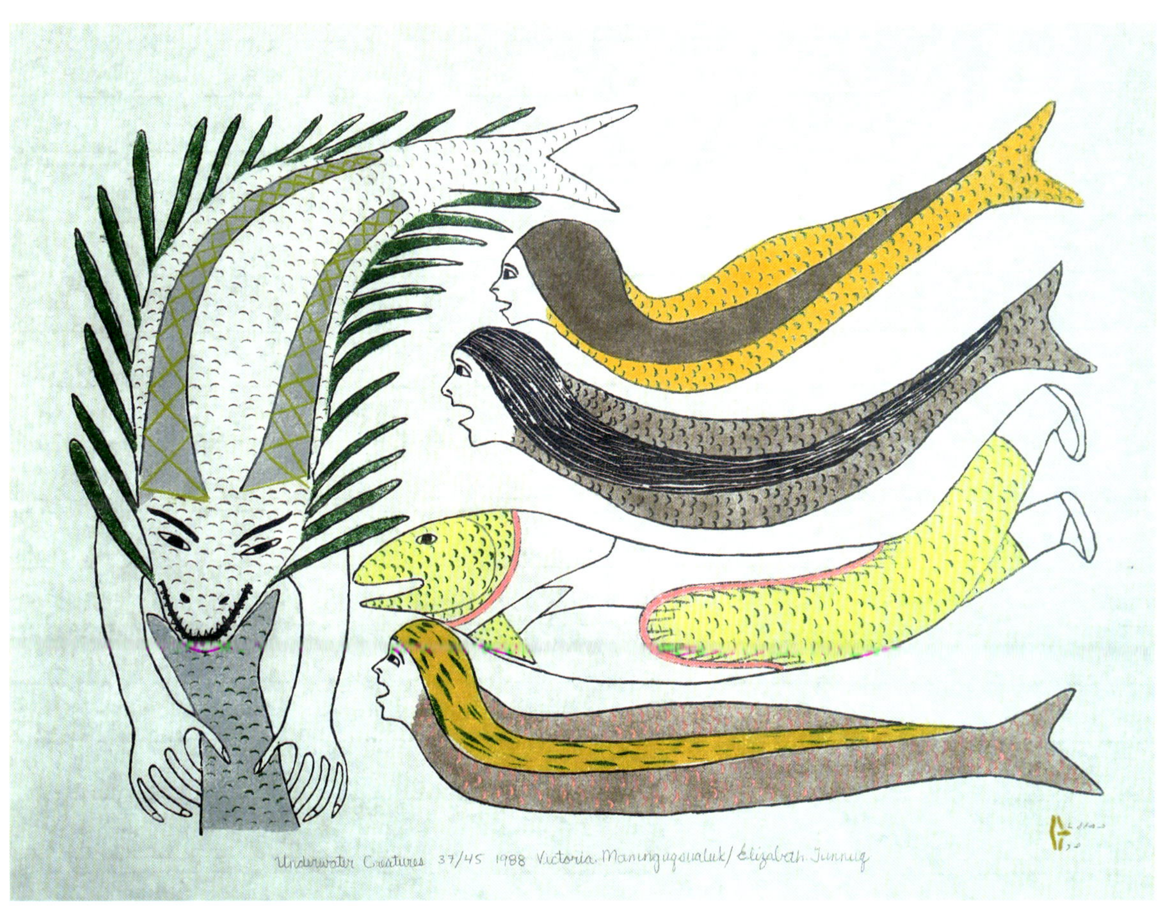

*Underwater Creatures*, 1988

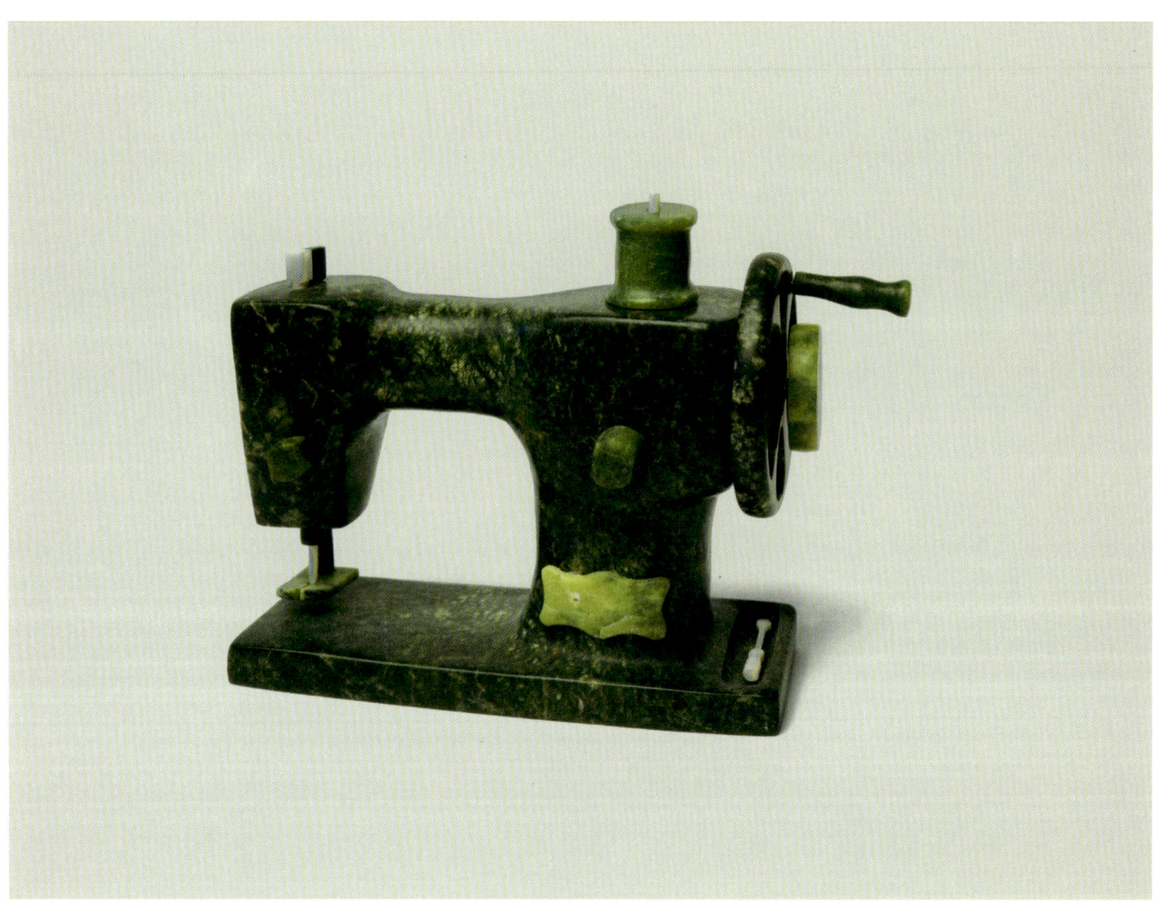

Jamasee Pitseolak, *Domestic Sewing Machine*, 2006

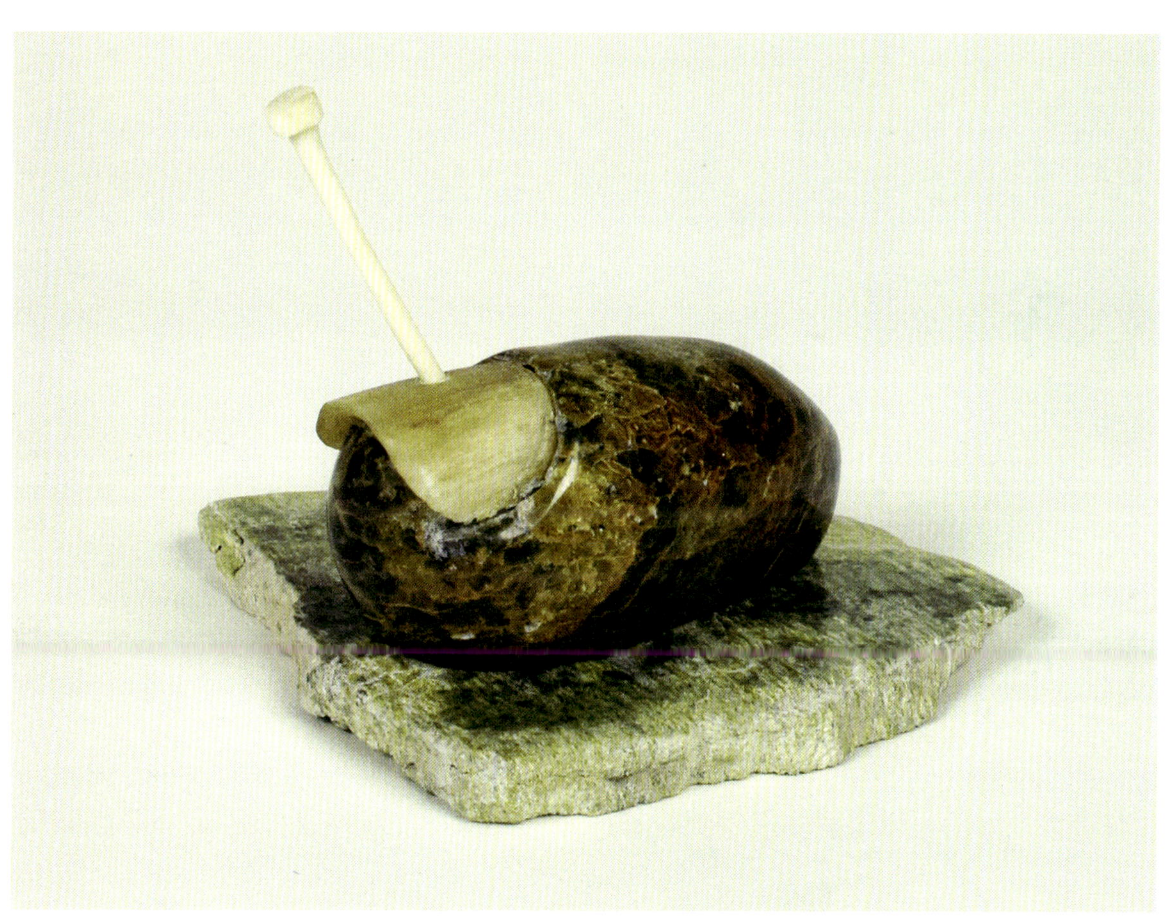

*Toe-Nailed*, 2006

Melissa Cody, *US*, 2016

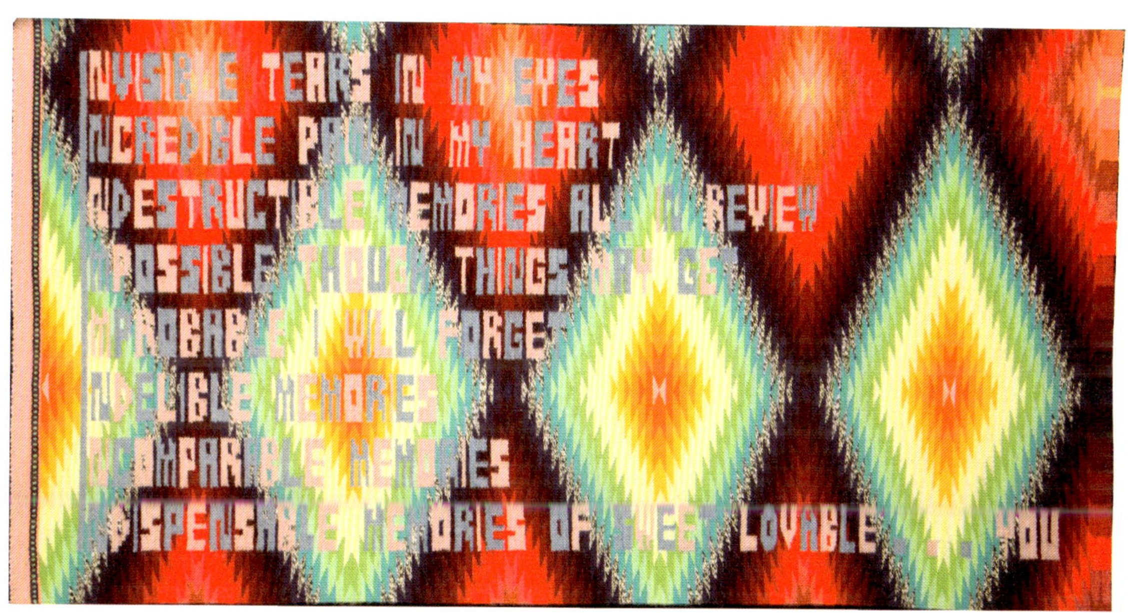


*Sweet lovable . . . You*, 2016

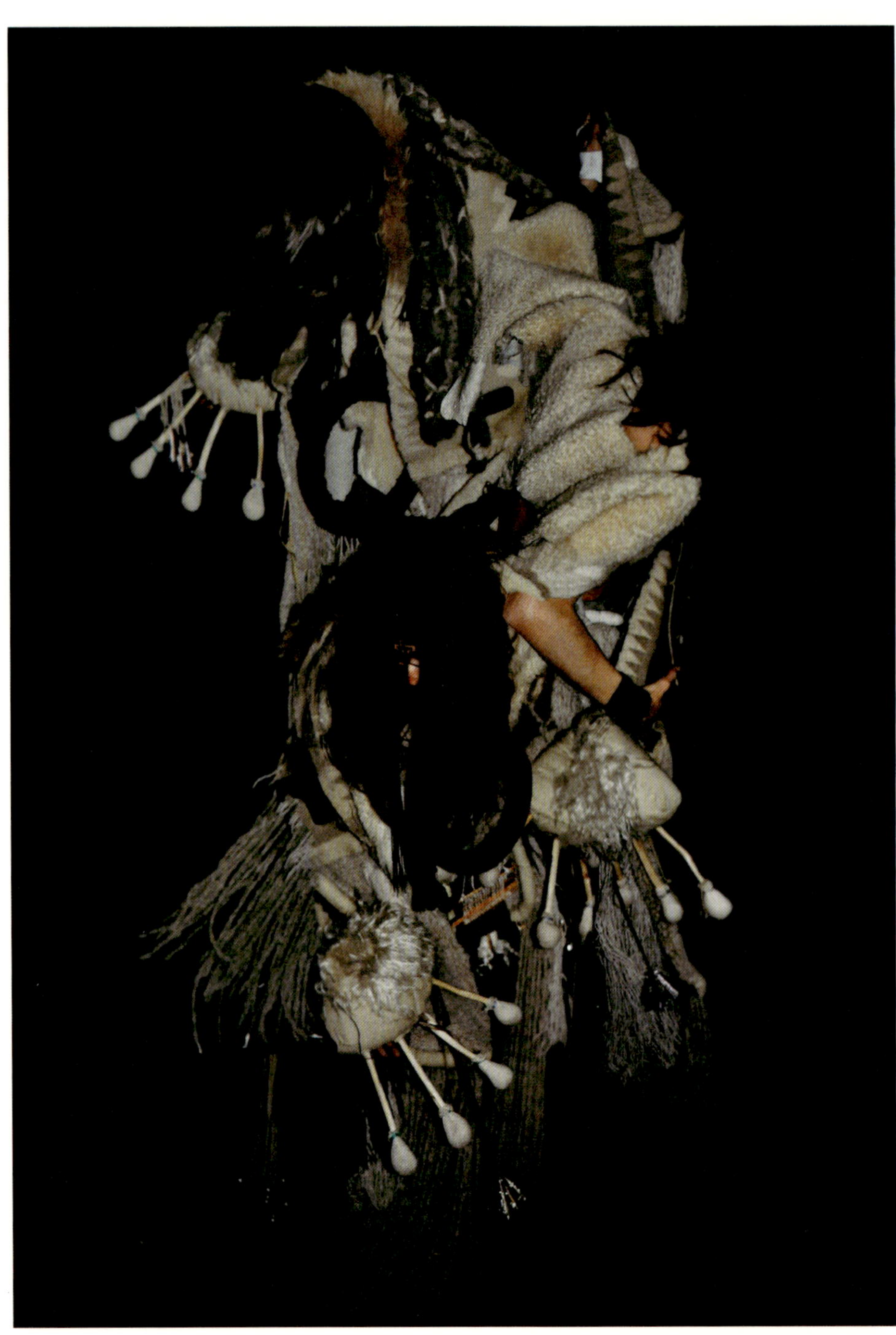

Eric-Paul Riege, studies for *diyin+, hooghan and weaving dance (fig.3)*
*for Na'ashjéíí Asdzáá, Retha, Effie, and Angela*, 2018

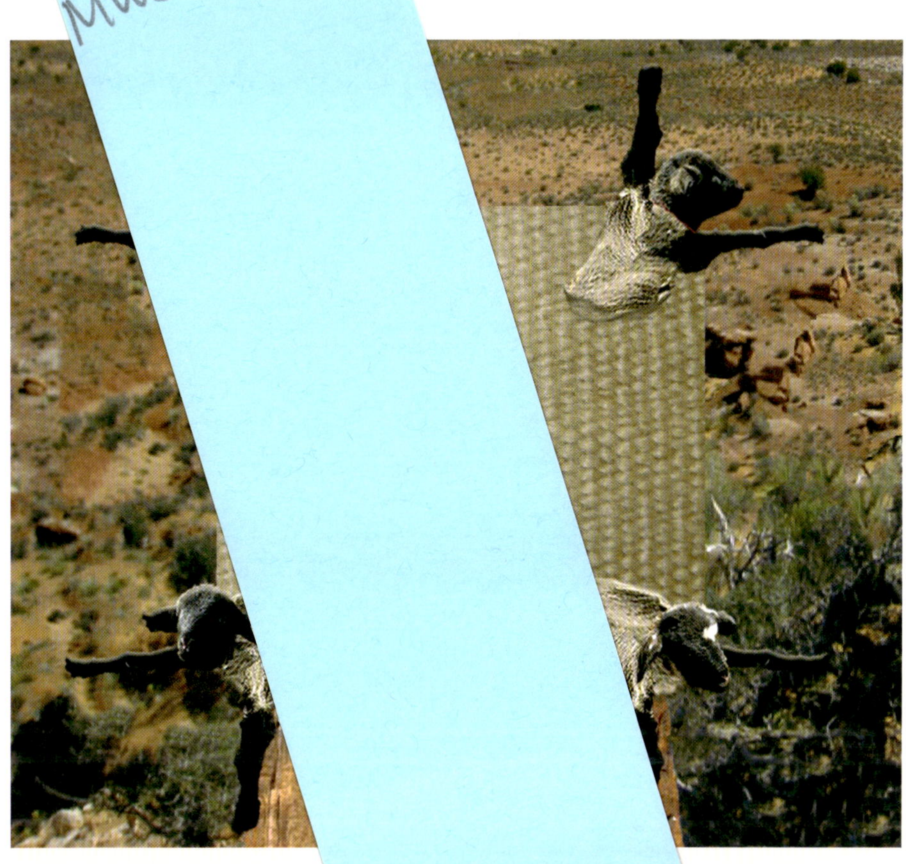

MW015 856


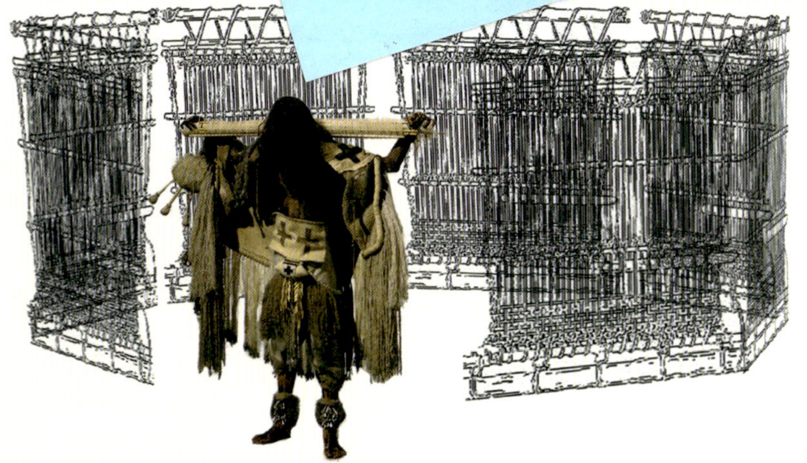

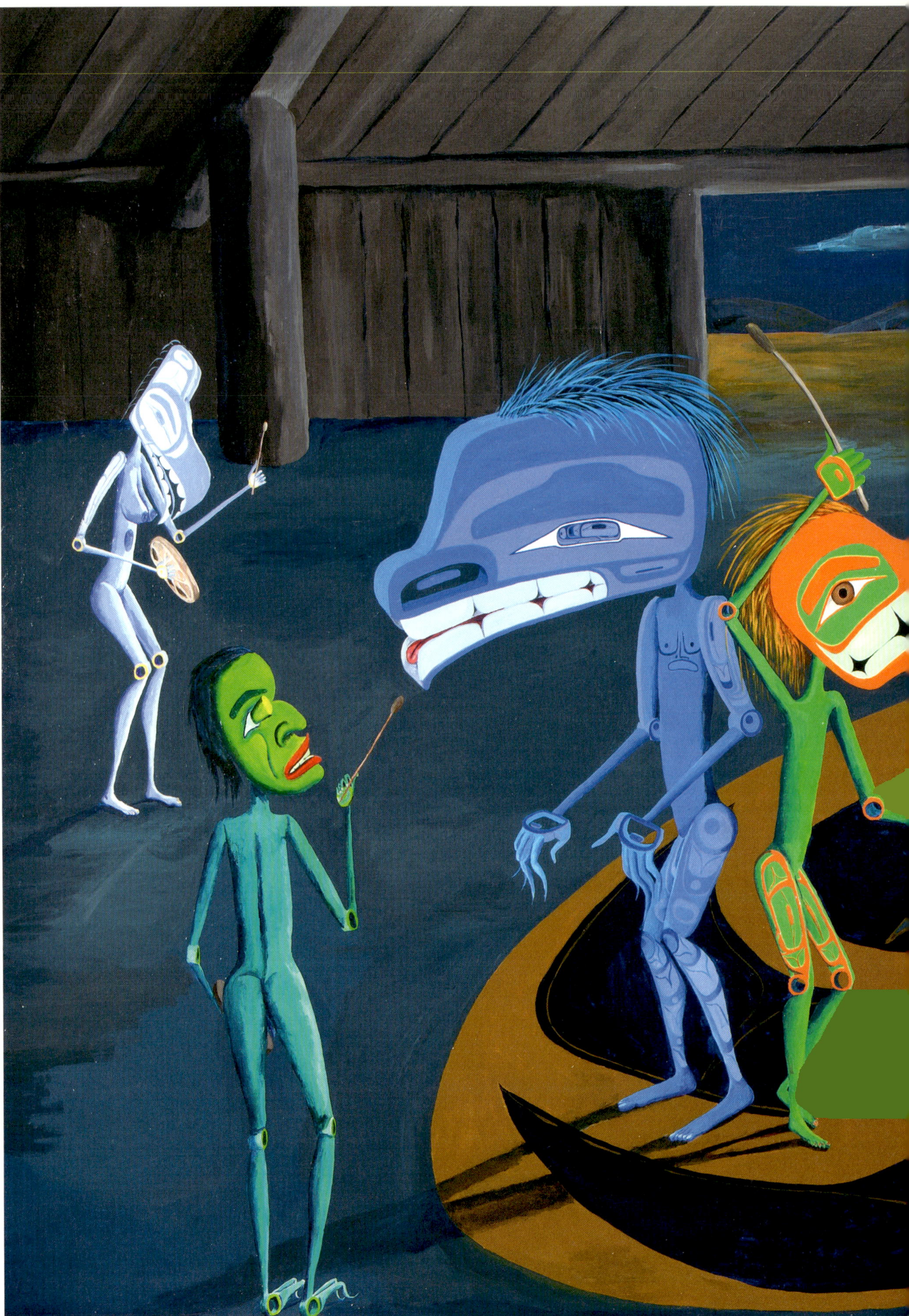

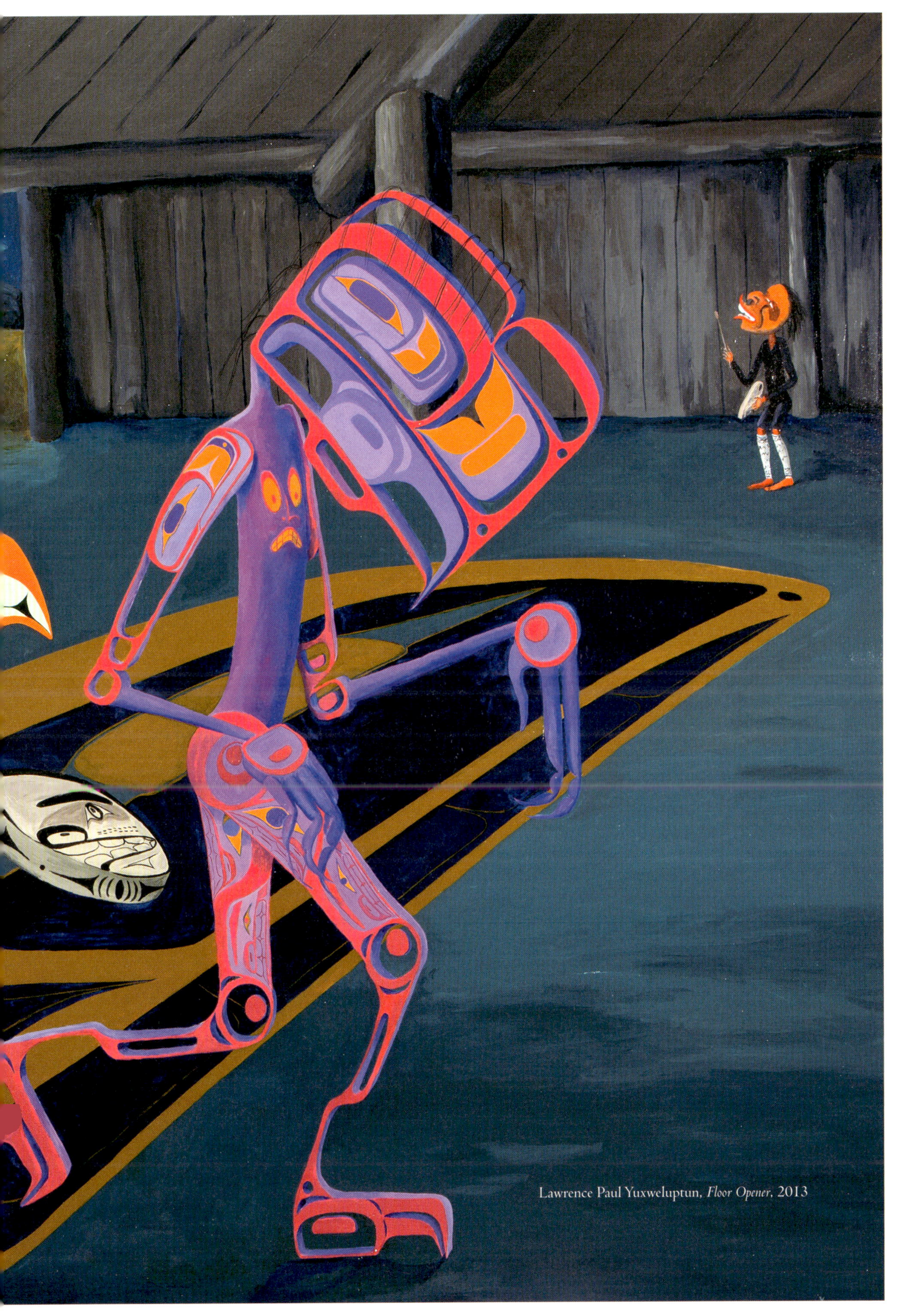

Lawrence Paul Yuxweluptun, *Floor Opener*, 2013

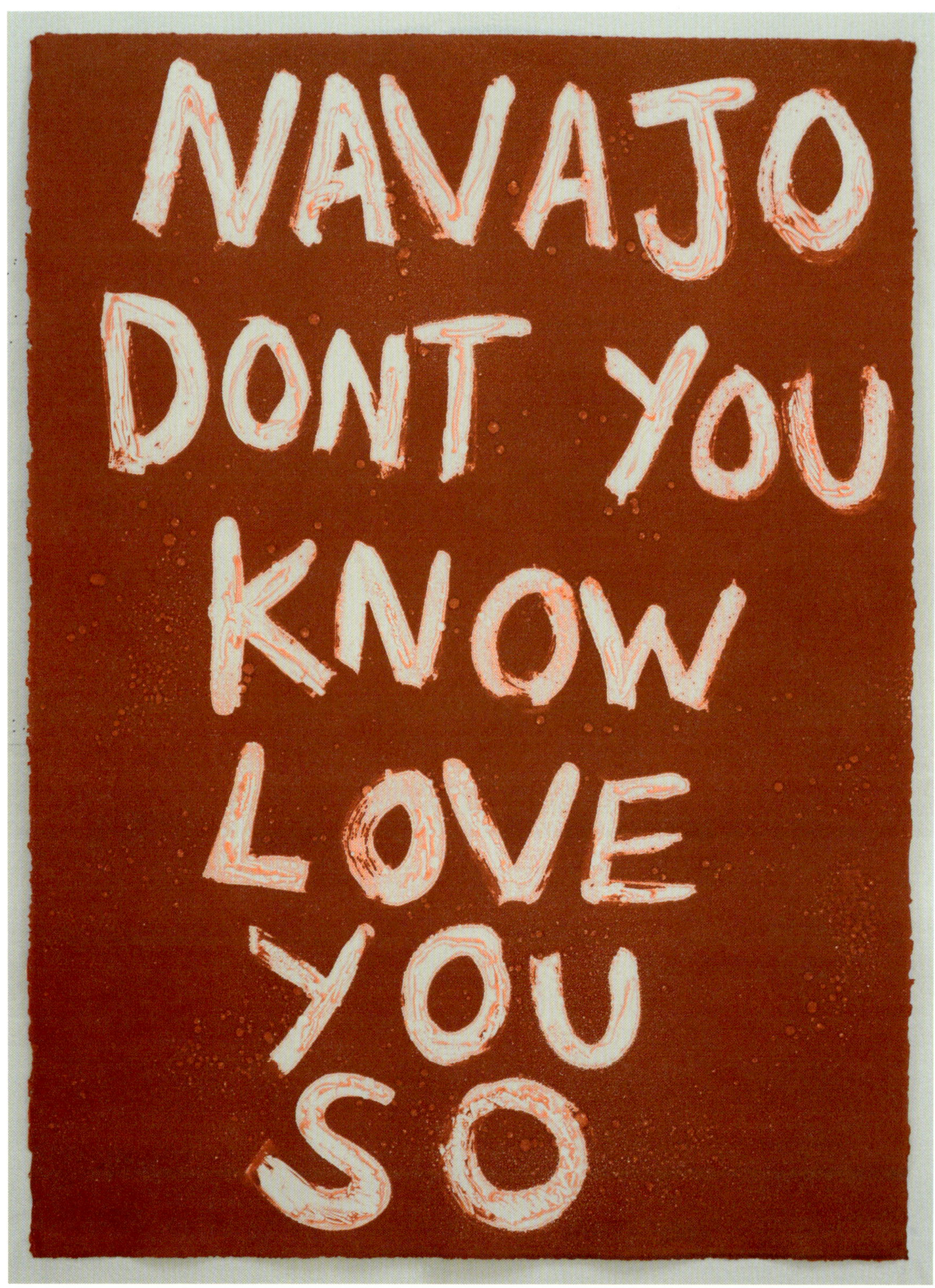


Hock E Aye Vi Edgar Heap of Birds, from the series *Surviving Active Shooter Custer*, 2018

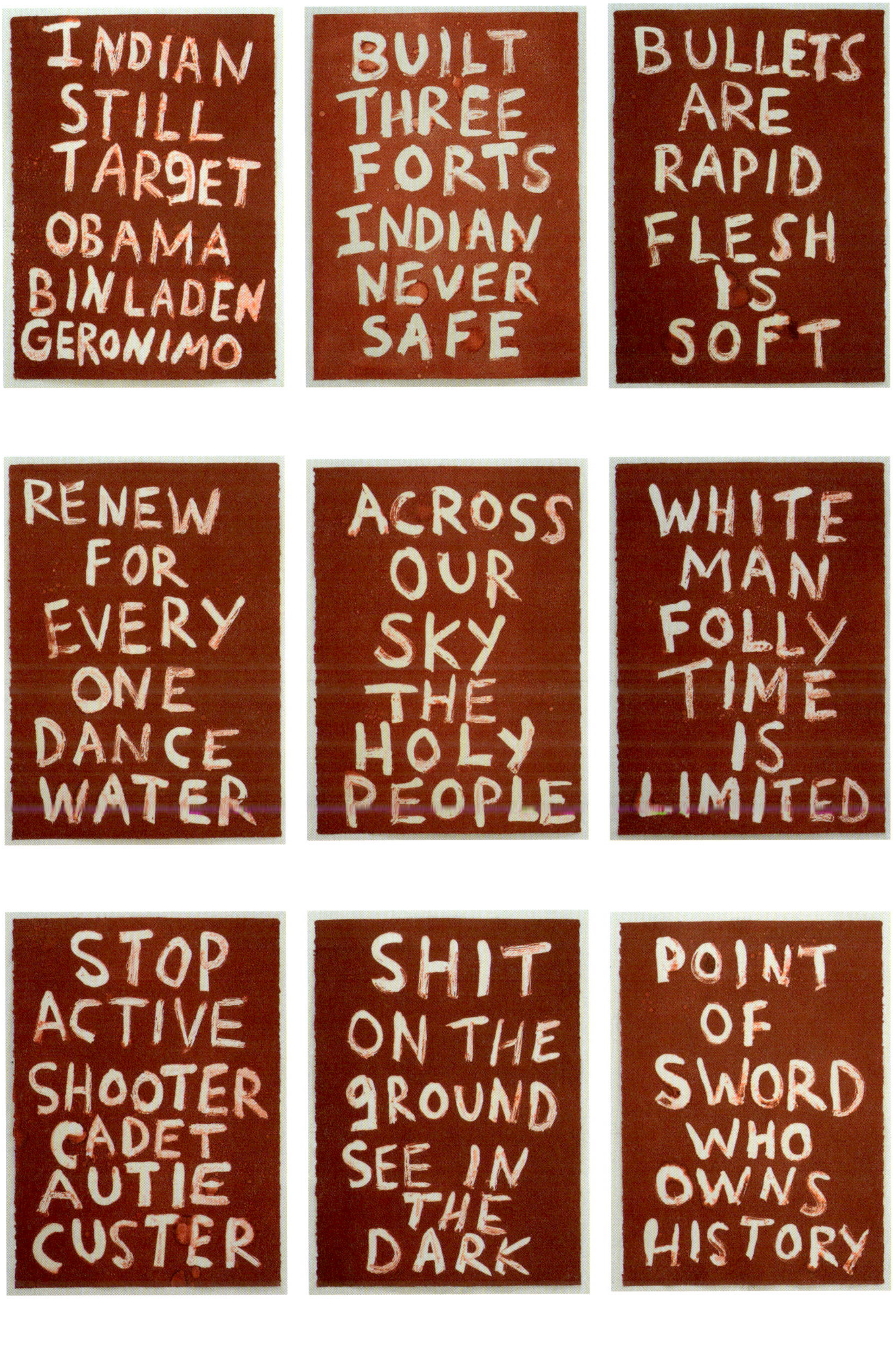

INDIAN
STILL
TARGET
OBAMA
BINLADEN
GERONIMO

BUILT
THREE
FORTS
INDIAN
NEVER
SAFE

BULLETS
ARE
RAPID
FLESH
IS
SOFT

RENEW
FOR
EVERY
ONE
DANCE
WATER

ACROSS
OUR
SKY
THE
HOLY
PEOPLE

WHITE
MAN
FOLLY
TIME
IS
LIMITED

STOP
ACTIVE
SHOOTER
CADET
AUTIE
CUSTER

SHIT
ON THE
GROUND
SEE IN
THE
DARK

POINT
OF
SWORD
WHO
OWNS
HISTORY

# DISPLACEMENTS

Ruba Katrib

It is striking how far the concept of home has moved from its meaning as a place of safety where people live, often with others, in neighborhoods where they form communities, alliances, and, inevitably, divisions. In a sobering assessment offered by sociologist David Madden and urban planner Peter Marcuse, there isn't a single state in the United States where a person who makes minimum wage and works full-time can afford to rent or buy a one-bedroom apartment or house.[1] The ability to call something your own has been undermined by a financial system that penalizes the poor. Home ownership is now only for the rich, even though the US and other nations demand ownership as a metric for good citizenship. The effects on human as well as animal populations that are pushed out of longtime homes and habitats have resulted in global catastrophe. Ironically, a chief factor contributing to home eviction and the destruction of habitat is residential and commercial development and its attendant needs (whose contribution to climate change results in further dislocation). As Madden and Marcuse point out, "in recent decades, residential displacement due to development, extraction, and construction has occurred on a scale that rivals displacement caused by disasters and armed conflicts."[2]

Under these conditions, the lower and even the middle class are portrayed as unequal citizens, or at least underperforming citizens. Prompting a social media uproar, the Treasury Secretary's wife recently claimed that she and her husband are superior to the average American because they have "given more to the economy" through their wealth.[3] Meanwhile, homelessness sky-rockets in most major cities, with the United Nations conducting an unprecedented investigation into poverty in the US, one of the wealthiest nations in the world.[4] It isn't just the cost of housing that contributes to disparities in prosperity and access to security, but also a reconfiguration of private and public spaces that has transformed how people occupy place. Disenfranchisement occurs through structural obstacles created to prevent citizens from achieving agency over their lives.

Place is an extension of self. While private property is a complex and debatable construct, to disconnect people from the basic comforts associated with a secure place to live has repercussions for the larger social order whatever it is. As a new global elite emerges, with the few owning more than the rest combined, inequities are rife. The monetizing of nearly everything and the virtualizing of value, no longer wrapped up in physical goods and materials, has abstracted the notion of home. What was once an affective concept has increasingly become simply a strategic investment, a place to park capital.[5] This has deep implications, as Eve Tuck and K. Wayne Yang have argued. Widespread assumptions, even on the part of leftist activists, that "land is property; land is/belongs to the US; land should be distributed democratically" means that "land can be owned by people" and that occupation is a right, a notion that reflects "a profoundly settling, anthropocentric, colonial view of the world."[6] Further, the growing virtual value system has had a significant role in usurping, redefining, and sometimes reinforcing the geographic center of local communities.

The shift in the siting of identity and culture from physical and geographical locations to abstracted and commercialized realms is a key concern of the exhibition *Casa tomada*. Displacement is a central issue for many of the participating artists—displacement from a location and from personal and cultural narratives—as is the fragmentation of culture in response to multifold global crises. The intrusion of the external world into the private domestic space, potentially leading to the ouster of its occupants, refuses people their

right to land, their right to community, their right to define for themselves their personal and social surroundings. In racialized social schemes such as housing projects, the home is under constant and visible police surveillance. Additionally, families can be physically separated by governmental laws, borders, and restrictive policies. In the US, the provisions of Deferred Action for Childhood Arrivals (DACA) are threatened by a volatile president who terrorizes people with draconion executive orders.[7] Immigrants are being detained for deportation in front of their children or trapped (including children) inside Immigration and Customs Enforcement (ICE) facilities for extended periods of time as they await admission or expulsion.[8]

Discussing the impact of US policies on drugs, gangs, violence, and displacement throughout the Americas, Valeria Luiselli argues that "to refer to the situation as a hemispheric war would be a step forward because it would oblige us to rethink the very language surrounding the problem and, in doing so, imagine potential directions for combined policies. But of course, a 'war refugee' is bad news and an uncomfortable truth for governments, because it obliges them to deal with the problem instead of simply 'removing the illegal aliens.'"[9] And as "aliens" are being denigrated and forcibly removed, Native lands and people are persistently trod on, often by corporations indifferent to the poisonous consequences of their actions (see the Dakota Access Pipeline). The insecurity of a claim to place goes beyond property to the question of survival and well-being. The artists represented in *Casa tomada* bring their specificities to bear on these broader issues, mapping what is at risk or in the process of being lost, and, in some cases, what it might take to move on.

Tania Pérez Córdova abstracts displacement, using formal and material choices to speak to identity formation, presence, and loss. Her *Blink*, 2017, is an attenuated marble column topped by a circular indentation filled with saline solution containing a single contact lens. Pérez Córdova's materials list sets the narrative frame for the work, providing guidance on what is there, what is happening, and what is not there. The lens, it is revealed, belongs to a specific person who exists outside the sculpture. The sculpture is not a portrait, but a sort of double or twin. Pérez Córdova's practice of leaving traces of people through and within static objects puts the body and its location into question. For one series, she creates mud forms that dry over a sustained period of time. In *Time-lapse*, 2017, a slab of earth "dried in the shade" and propped up like a tombstone contains "makeup, cigarette butt, plastic wrapping, Mexican 50-peso note." The materials, all of which were once in intimate contact with the body, are human-made detritus that literally colors this terra-based document of people, time, and place. The durational aspect of the work is embedded in its surface.

For *Placebo*, 2017, Pérez Córdova has cast in aluminum a hole she discovered in the ground. The negative space on display in the gallery corresponds to an originary place elsewhere. Rising out of the metal cavity, fourteen gold necklaces, all but one of them fake, are linked together and hooked to the ceiling. The identity of the real gold necklace is indecipherable, indicated only by the materials list, casting the authenticity of the whole group into doubt. By drawing a line from the "ground" to the ceiling, Pérez Córdova unites two distinct geographical realms, and by juxtaposing common costume with rare "real" jewelry, she insinuates a distinction of value. Enacting situations and evoking actions, Pérez Córdova's works are haunted by what is implied but unverifiable.

Place, fragmentation, historical events, imagined scenes, personal narratives, and state-sanctioned violence inform the work of Curtis Talwst Santiago (a former apprentice of Lawrence Paul Yuxweluptun, also represented in the exhibition). Since 2008, Santiago has built dioramas in what he refers to as "reclaimed" jewelry boxes. He launched his *Infinity Series* by carrying such boxes in his pockets as a sort of portable artwork to show people he met. Since 2010, they have been displayed in gallery and museum shows.

In the current exhibition, Santiago presents a massive collection of the boxes, broaching the encyclopedic, in a room custom-built within the space. The imagery contained within the boxes ranges from portraits to historical happenings, landscapes, references to art history, scenes from daily life, and events from different parts of the world and points in time. *Frida's Entry into Iguala*, 2015, refers to the ongoing protests against the forced disappearance of forty-three Mexican students in 2014 at the hands of a confederation of local police, military personnel, and drug cartels, and relates the tragedy to a James Ensor painting. In *The Execution of Michael Brown*, 2014, the artist restages the killing of an unarmed teenager by police in Ferguson, Missouri, that same year. Instructive and illustrative, his boxes both protect and conceal the moments inside, which, frozen in place, are also historicized as dioramas. While miniaturization should make troubling scenes more manageable, the scale does nothing to diminish the impact of war, racism, violence, or sexism; in fact, they become more troubling through their proposed intimacy. Other works in the series are more tender, such *Zulu Mother and Child*, 2017, and portraits or art-historical scenes that become undetermined and untethered monuments. The culture the works produce is different from the civic context that historical monuments traditionally engage; they instead evoke proximity and privacy, as well as the limits of memorialization and preservation.

Jumana Manna's film *Wild Relatives*, 2018, addresses another sort of container meant to preserve materials—the seed bank. The work is focused on the first extraction of seeds, in 2015, from the Svalbard Seed Vault, a "doomsday vault" located between Norway and the North Pole, for transport to the Bekaa Valley in Lebanon. Through this movement of materials, the film examines a little-publicized consequence of the war in Syria. Syria is an agricultural country, and before the war many varieties of seeds from the region, as well as other dry climates, were stored at the International Center for Agricultural Research in the Dry Areas (ICARDA) outside Aleppo. Once the city was under siege, the Center had to relocate to Lebanon and was forced to leave the seeds behind. The seeds represent not only heritage and culture, but the very survival of humans and other species. Violent conflict has added a universal threat to essential crops already at risk due to the dominance of monocultures and genetic modification. Ironically, the biotechnologies destructive of heirloom crops also offer hope for their preservation. To create a backup of the backup in Syria, ICARDA is replicating the seeds that were brought from the Svalbard Seed Vault. Manna's film shows a group of young women from Syria who now work on the farms in Lebanon where the seeds are grown and replicated. The women are seemingly unaware of the significance of their activity; happy for the work, they chat about their favorite recipes, smoke cigarettes, and do a *dabke*—a traditional dance from the Levant region. Manna also speaks to a Syrian farmer living in Lebanon who has created his own low-fi heritage seed bank in a shed, much in contrast to the secure Svalbard Seed Vault chilled to -18° Celsius. In another scene, a landowner argues that it makes more economic sense for him to rent out his land for refugee camps than to continue farming it: the importation of produce has created unbeatable competition. Meanwhile, his father's attachment to the land is seen as a relationship irretrievably lost to younger generations.

Through these narratives, *Wild Relatives* addresses preservationist strategies that prepare for the unthinkable at a time when the unthinkable is occurring more and more often. Human efforts to save seeds, and thus culture, for a better day makes assurances that all is not lost, that resurrection is possible. But the current state of affairs rattles the confidence that the recreation of the past, or even the present, will be viable at any time in the future. And further, who is and will be undertaking such efforts? The displacement of seeds central to the film is paralleled by the displacement of people. The growing domination of commercial investment in the genetic engineering of crops threatens personal claims to the land. The vault is a Noah's Ark that may not prove seaworthy.

With his outdoor sculpture *Galactic Playground*, 2018, Eduardo Navarro has created a large-scale interactive game board based on the cycles of the sun. Like a brightly colored spaceship that has landed in Santa Fe for a six-month visit, Navarro's work is activated by the cosmos. As in a sundial, the shadow of a gnomon moves through a sequence of instructions written on a large hexagonal concrete surface as the sun appears to move across the sky. The instructions, then, vary according to the time of day and the season. Some trigger a physical action, others conceptual considerations, and all connect the player with the sun as well as with other living entities. Predictable in its movements yet constantly shifting in its qualities, the work reminds the viewer of the extreme distance in time and space between itself and the force that activates it. The gulf between the sun and the player is reduced by the awareness that all life is dependent on solar energy. The indispensable sun creates the rules and timeline of the game, which, however, is available to be played at any time, by anyone or anything.

Notions around the "alien" in the exhibition are troubled in terms of who does and does not belong, and how this is determined. In Navarro's work, people may play the game, but nature also plays people. In Pérez Córdova's works, objects perform people and places, and in Manna's work native seeds are preserved by the same biotechnologies that have put them at risk. Scenes are turned into micro-monuments untethered from local contexts: from Santiago's works to the altered Oñate monument discussed by Naomi Beckwith in this catalogue (pages 123–27), the exhibition considers multiple instances of questionable memorials. One such icon is Lutz Bacher's large-scale print of a space rocket separated into segments, which runs like a giant banner across the exterior of the SITE Santa Fe building. The photograph could have been taken at the Kennedy Space Center, or Cape Canaveral, which is part space station, part museum, and part amusement park. The rocket is a symbol of exploration, scientific advancement, and, as a central feature of the military–industrial complex, imperialism. In the image, the decommissioned rocket is installed in a park, on display to visitors dwarfed by its scale. The museological function of the engineering marvel is emphasized in the SITE installation, as if the building had been temporarily transformed into a different kind of cultural institution.

Another work by Bacher on view is a classroom whiteboard inscribed with key words and topics from American history, such as "Ho Chi Minh," "Iron Curtain," and "Montgomery Bus Boycott." Elsewhere on the board someone has written "summer" and a date has been set for a "DJ party." Parts of words are missing, some are filled in, others have been added by students. Fragmented terms form an incomprehensible whole. The board as an art-work embodies a lesson about the construction of education as well as the national and global impact of imperialism. Embedded within each of the terms is an intricate and sprawling web of cause and effect contributing to the global condition that contemporary culture must grapple with.

In her video *Men Who Swallow Themselves in Mirrors*, 2017, Sable Elyse Smith plays with representations of masculinity as captured with personal handheld cameras and in commercial footage. Scenes include a cellphone recording of a man getting into an argument on the New York subway, video diaries made by the artist's father, excerpts from music videos and movies, and the first scene of the 1968 *Powers of Ten*, a film by Charles and Ray Eames concerning the relative scale of the universe. The work touches on the criminalization of Black men, who account for the majority of prison populations, whatever their crime.[10] As Smith argues in this work and others, the state plays an active part in the construction of American family life. By inserting her own history into the narrative framework, Smith complicates the construction of images of race and masculinity in relation to violence. At one point, her father talks about her discovery as a child that he owned a gun. He reminisces about the episode, lovingly, from a jail cell. Smith interweaves her father's recorded messages with mainstream material, images of other men who are not her father, guns that are not his guns. And within this construct, she relates the scale of the individual human being to that of the cosmos.

The artists represented in the exhibition, and not only the ones highlighted here, speak to notions of displacement and removal. Their works are troubling reminders of spaces and histories outside the exhibition site—they scale down and up their references and

narratives from the micro to the macro.
Missing parts, filled-in holes and boxes,
the movement of people and things, and
the sequestration of information and identity
all speak to the growing alienation of people
and other living things from place, land,
and community. Specific methodologies of
material and representational investigations
speak to possible recoveries of what has been
lost. The house, the ship, the vault, the cell,
the playground, the box, the hole, and the
classroom are vehicles for the sharing of
individual stories. And maybe not all built
to last, but certainly all built to move.

## ENDNOTES

1. David Madden and Peter Marcuse, *In Defense of Housing* (London: Verso, 2016), 2.

2. Ibid., 3.

3. Louise Linton, quoted in Damian Paletta, "Treasury Secretary's Wife Boasts of Travel on Government Plane, Touts Hermes and Valentino," *Washington Post* Wonkblog, August 21, 2017, https://www.washingtonpost.com/news/wonk/wp/2017/08/21/treasury-secretarys-wife-boasts-of-travel-on-government-plane-touts-hermes-and-valentino-fashion/?noredirect=on&utm_term=.b0041c2c9316.

4. Philp Alston, introduction to "Extreme Poverty in America: UN Special Monitor's Report," *Guardian* online, December 15, 2017, https://www.theguardian.com/world/2017/dec/15/extreme-poverty-america-un-special-monitor-report.

5. It is notable that a real estate investor is currently president of the United States.

6. Tuck and Yang point to settler tendencies in the Occupy movement's rhetoric, in Eve Tuck and K. Wayne Yang, "Decolonization Is Not a Metaphor," *Decolonization: Indigeneity, Education & Society* 1, no. 1 (2012): 24.

7. Sudhin Thanawala, "First Appeals Court to Weigh Trump's Decision to End DACA," *Chicago Tribune* online, May 15, 2018, http://www.chicagotribune.com/news/nationworld/politics/ct-trump-daca-immigration-20180515-story.html.

8. See Valeria Luiselli, *Tell Me How It Ends: An Essay in Forty Questions* (Minneapolis: Coffee House Press, 2017).

9. Ibid., 86–87.

10. Angela Y. Davis, *Are Prisons Obsolete?* (New York: Seven Stories Press, 2003), 113.

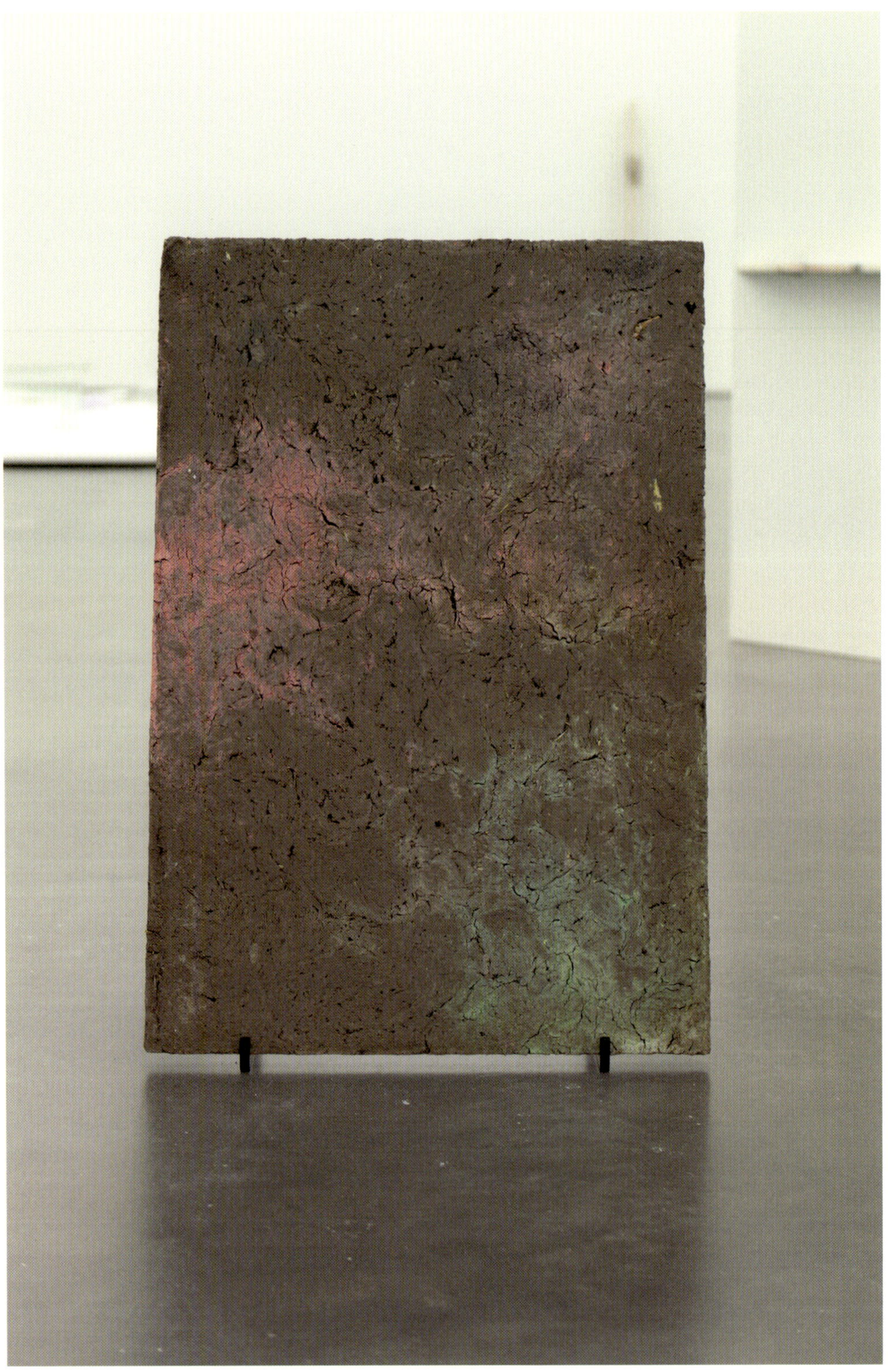

Tania Pérez Córdova, *Time-lapse*, 2017

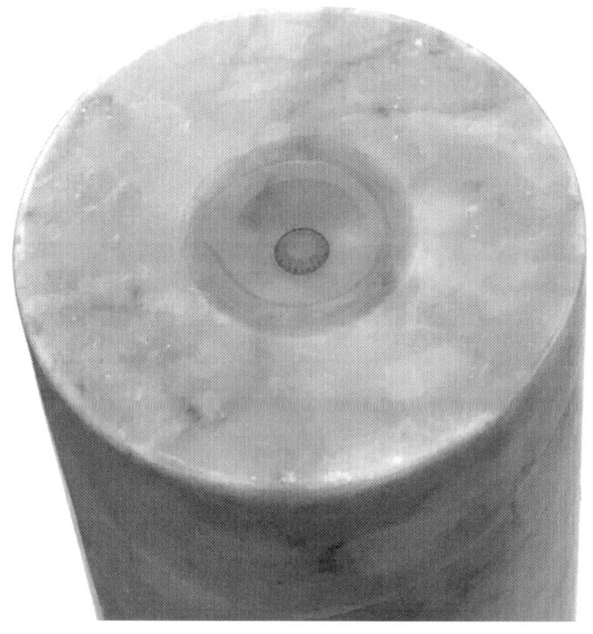

*Blink*, 2017

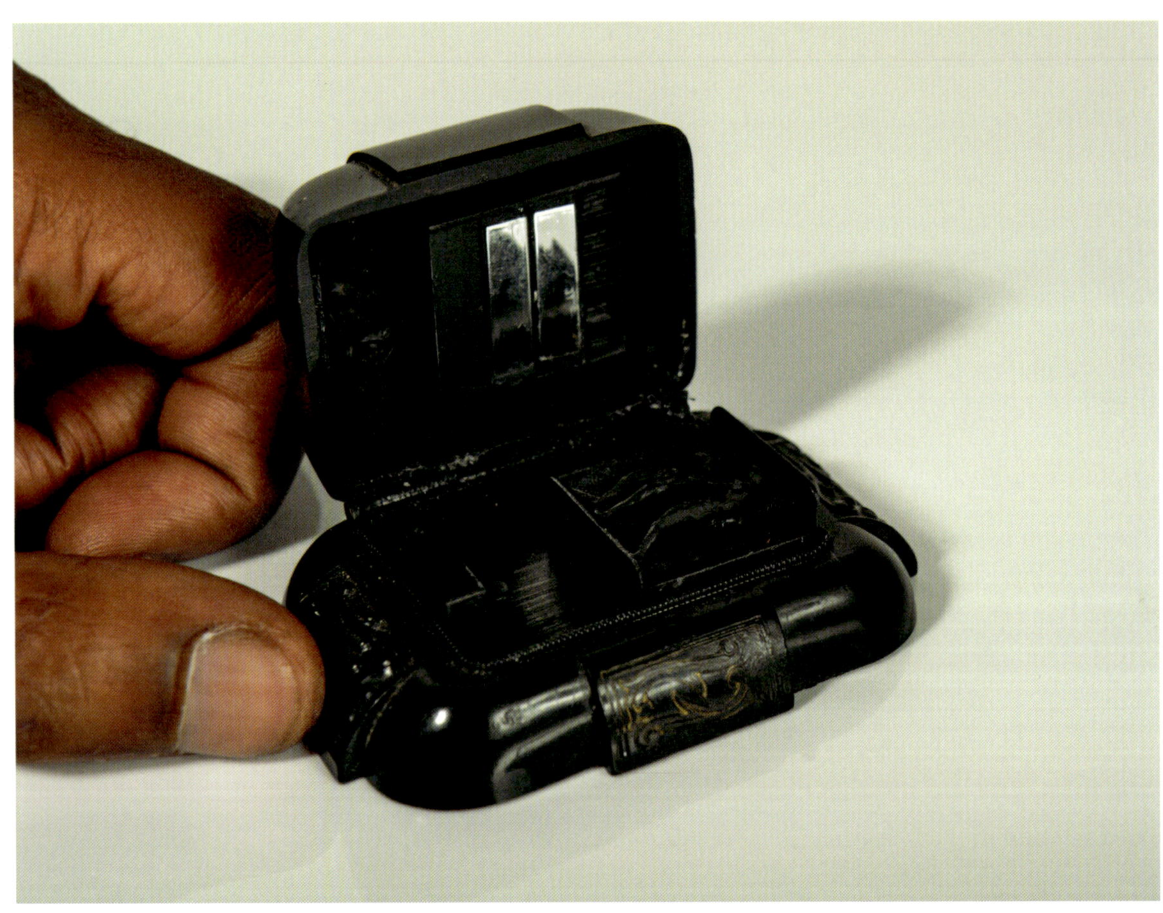

Curtis Talwst Santiago, *Black Knights*, 2014, from *Infinity Series*, 2008–ongoing

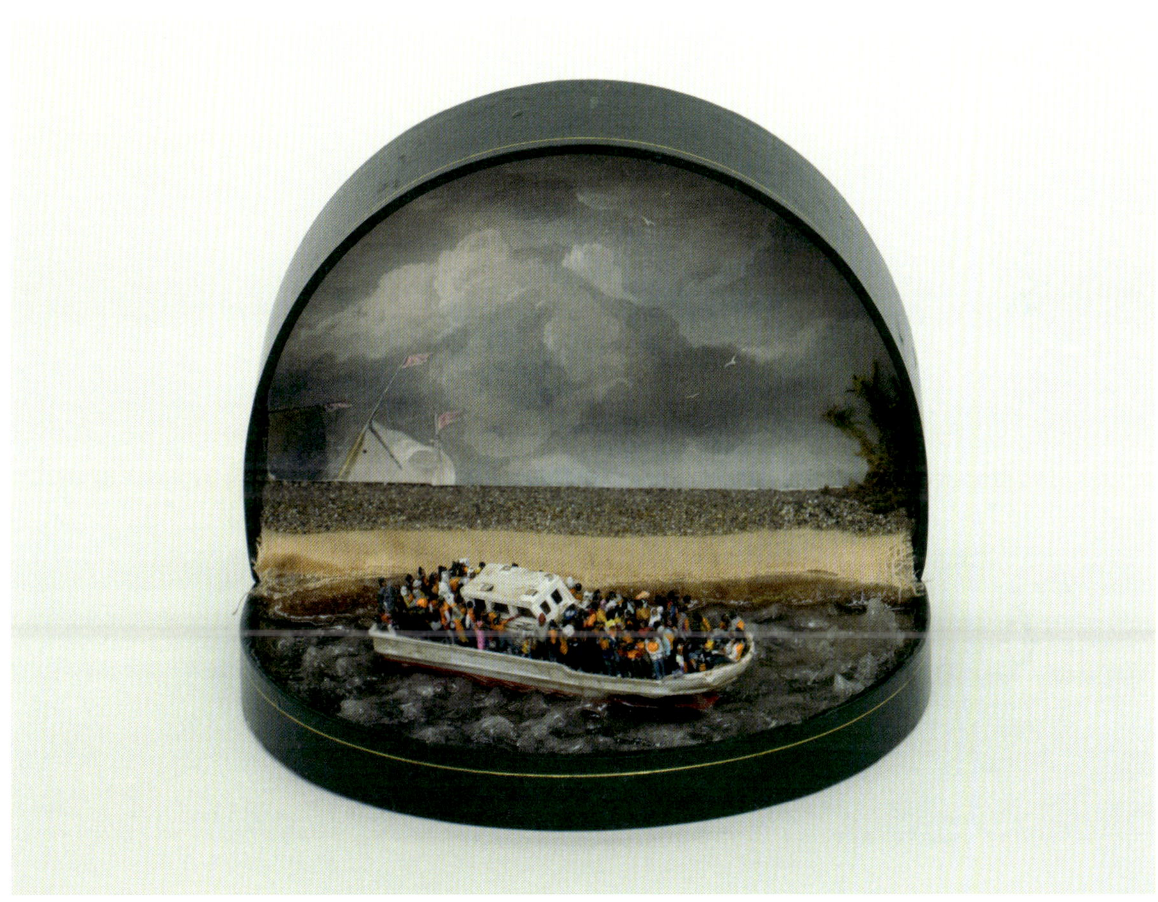

*Deluge VII*, 2016, from *Infinity Series*, 2008–ongoing

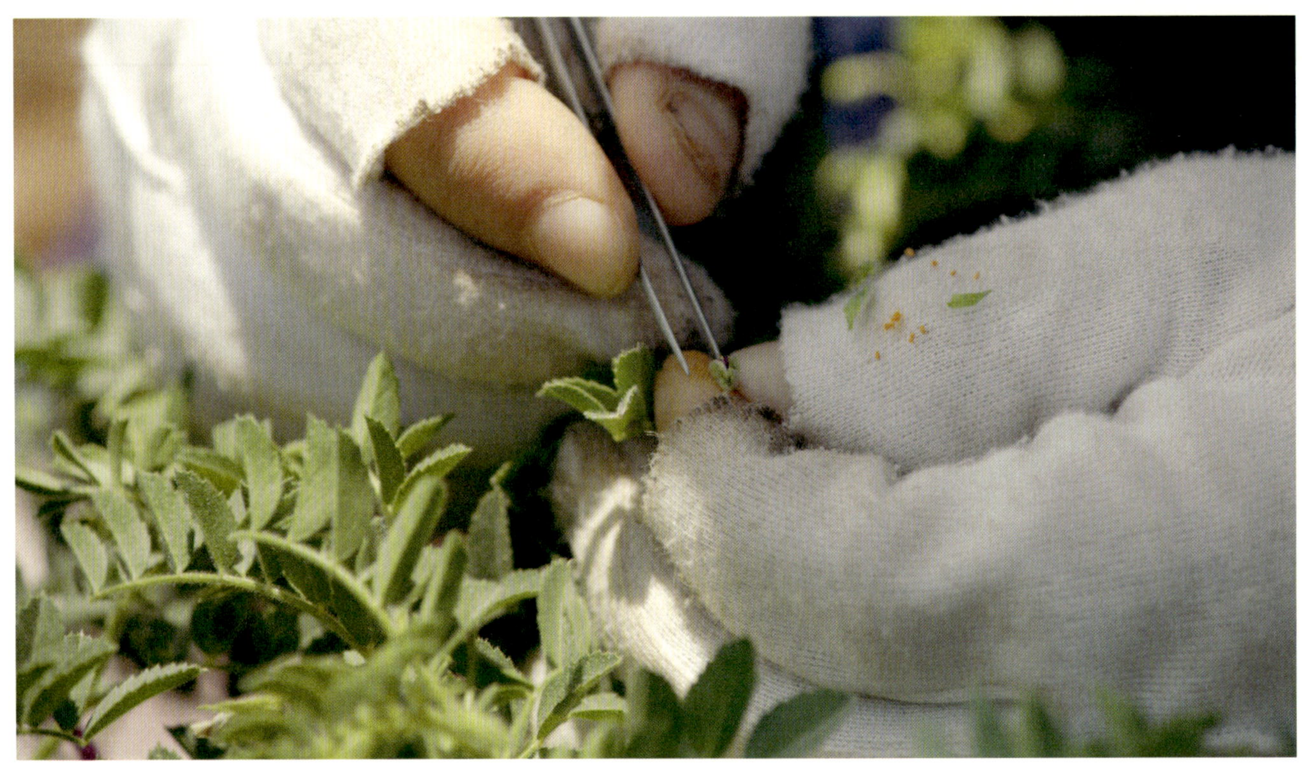

Jumana Manna, *Wild Relatives*, 2018 (stills)

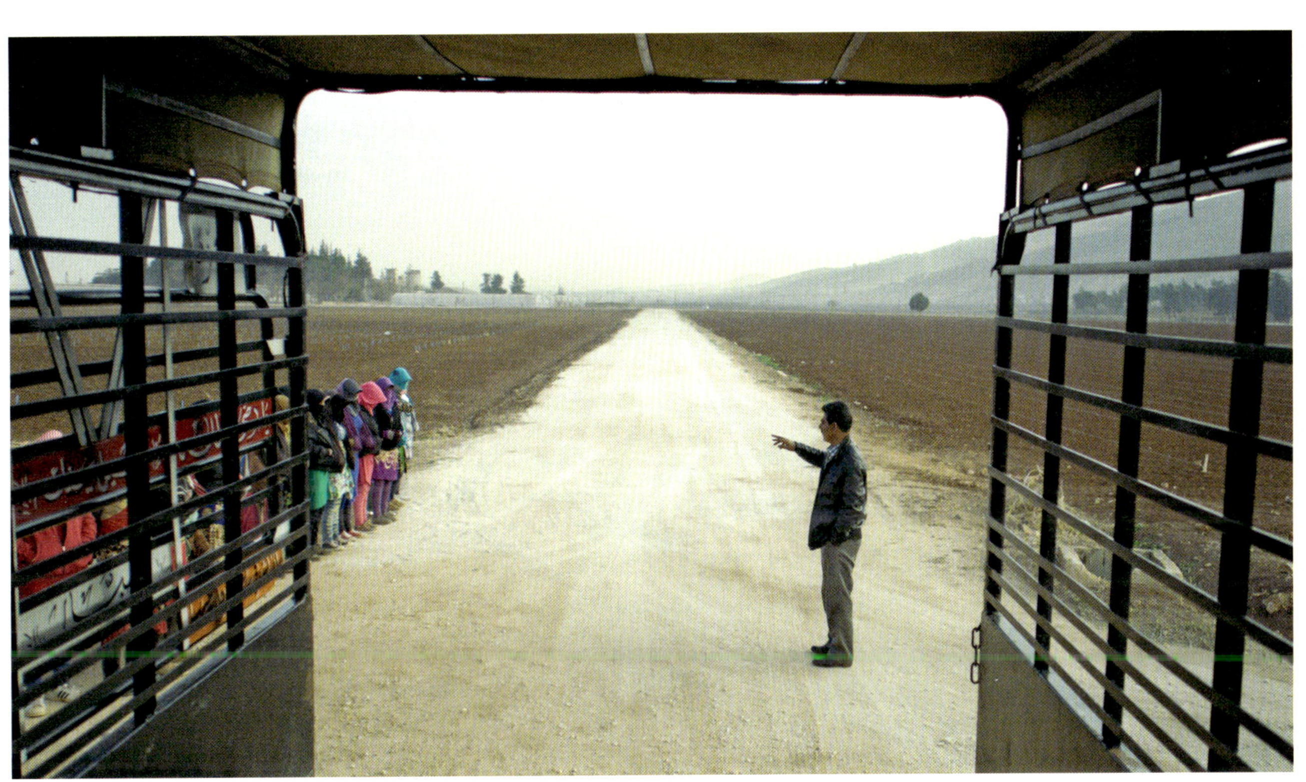

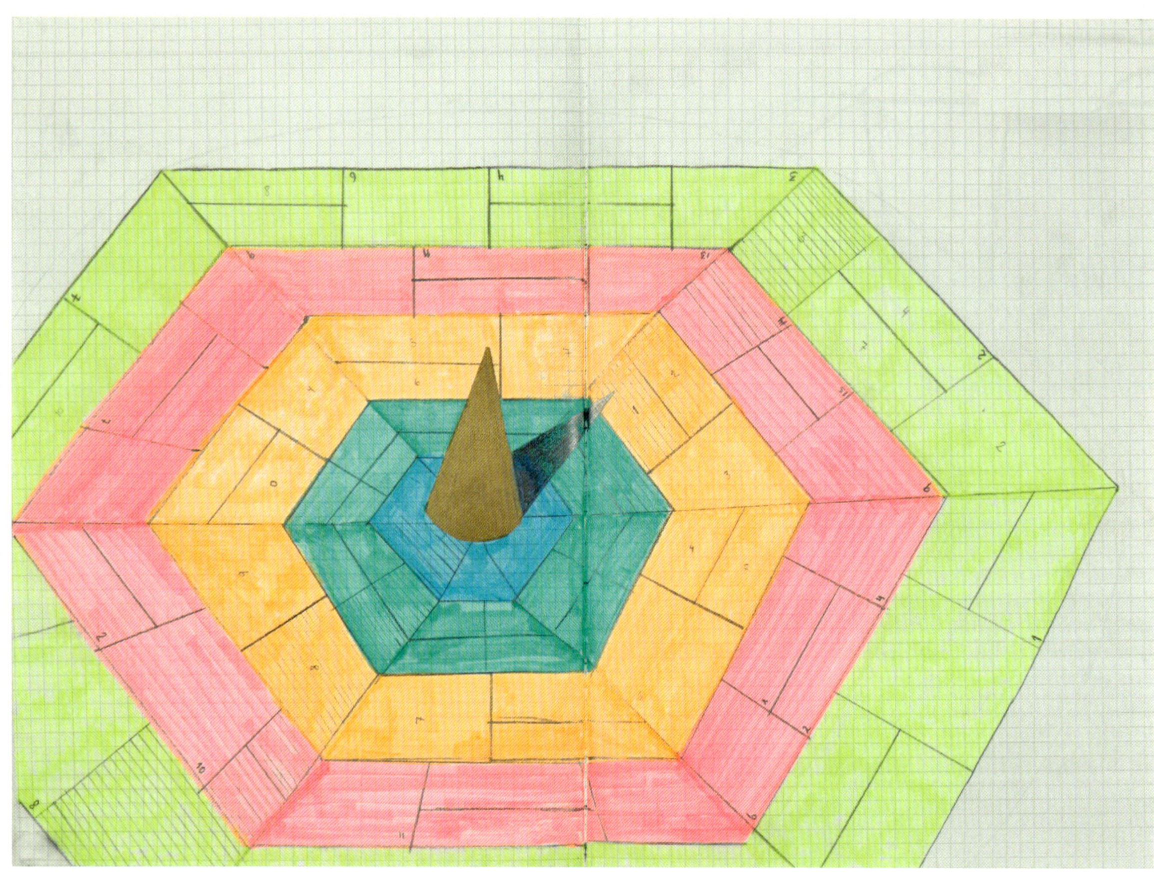

Eduardo Navarro, studies for *Galactic Playground*, 2018

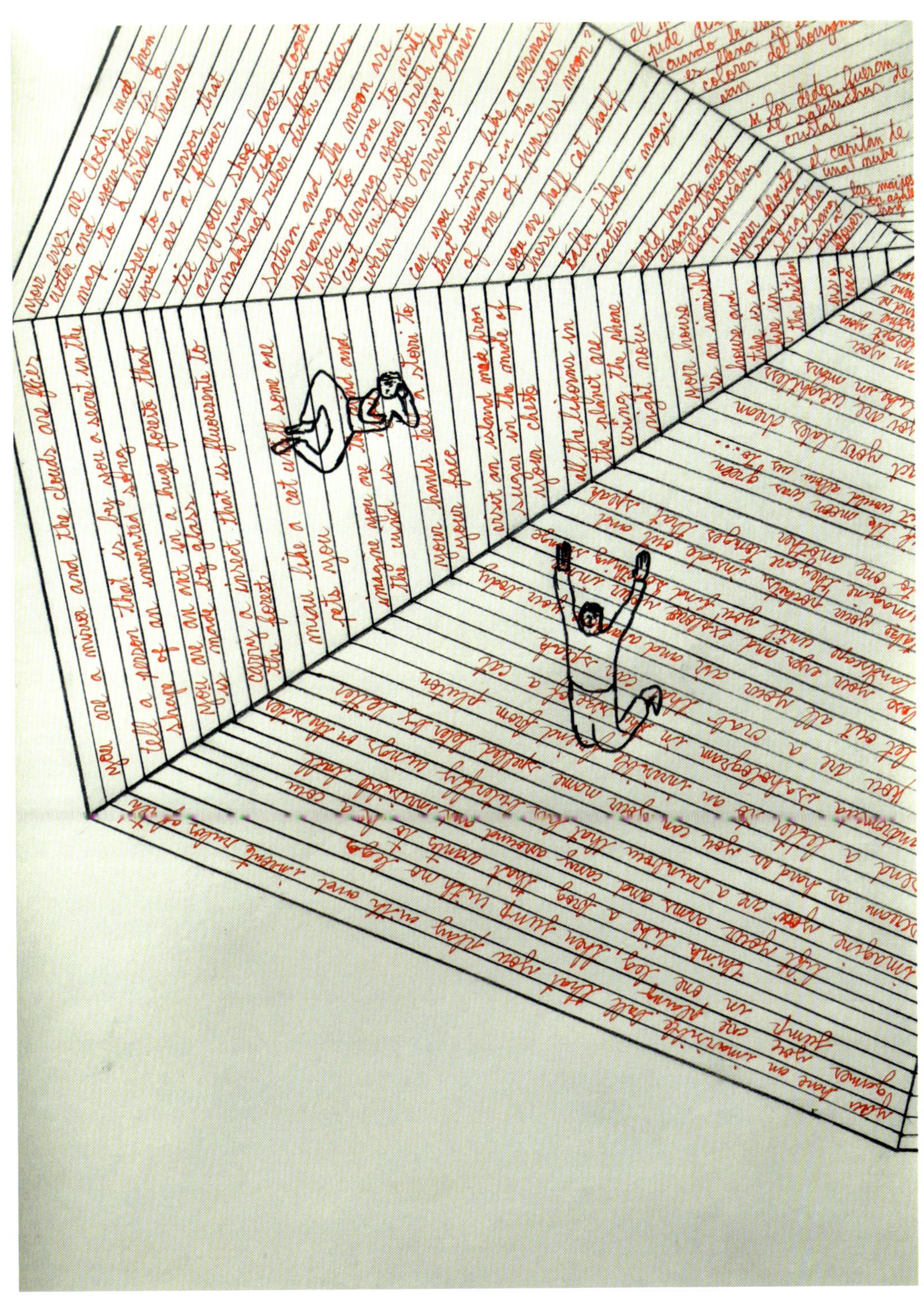

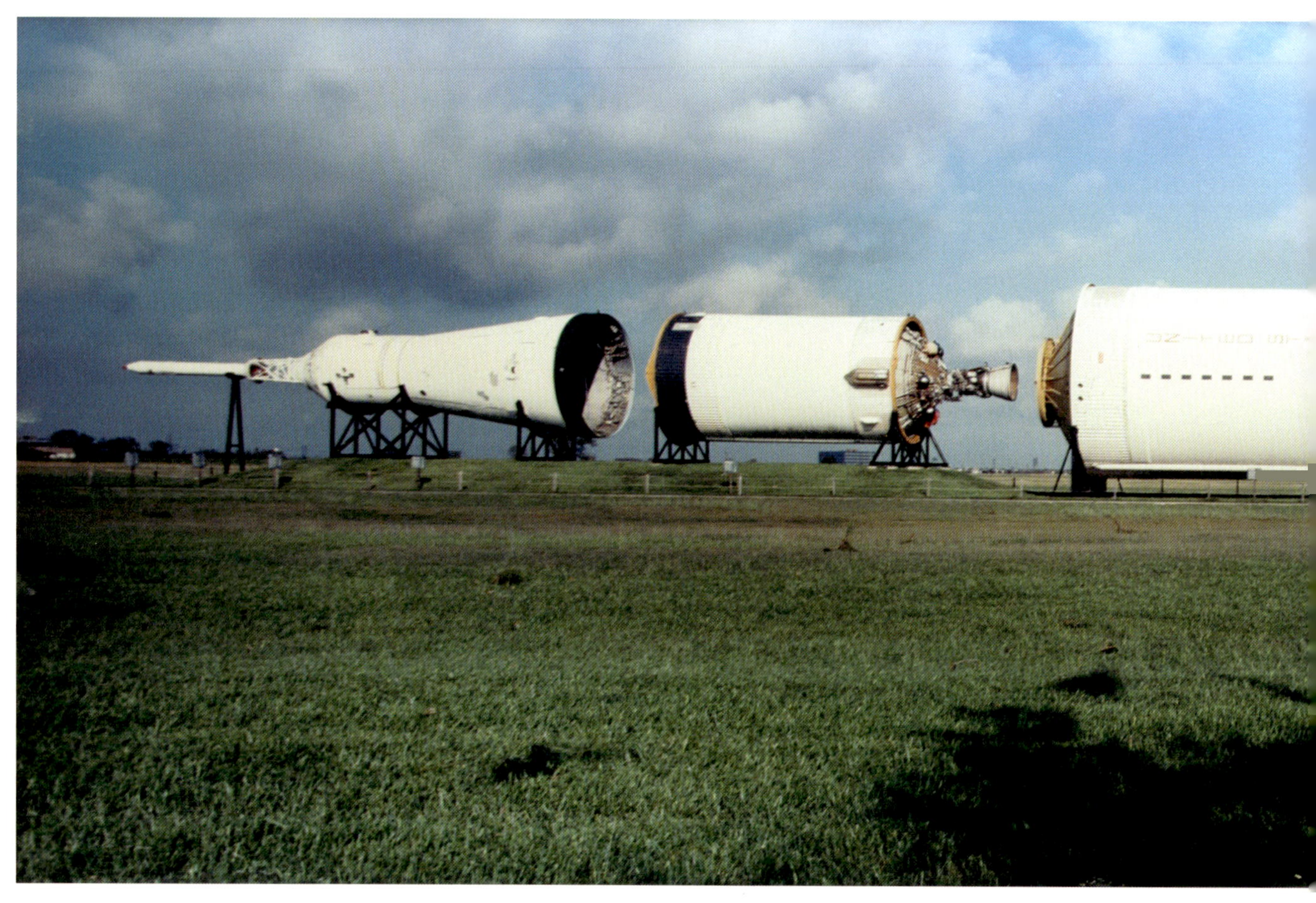

Lutz Bacher, *Rocket*, 2016–18

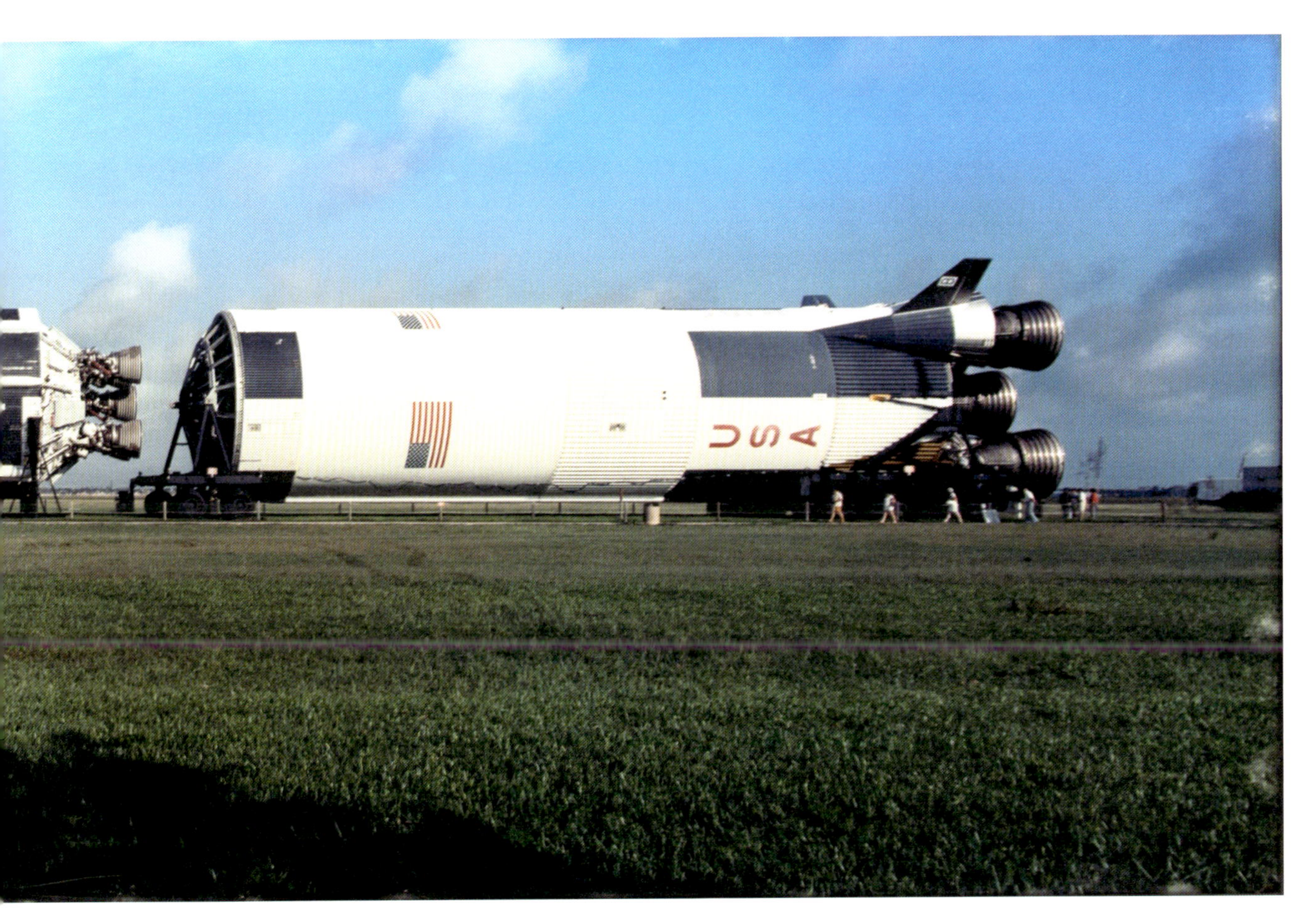

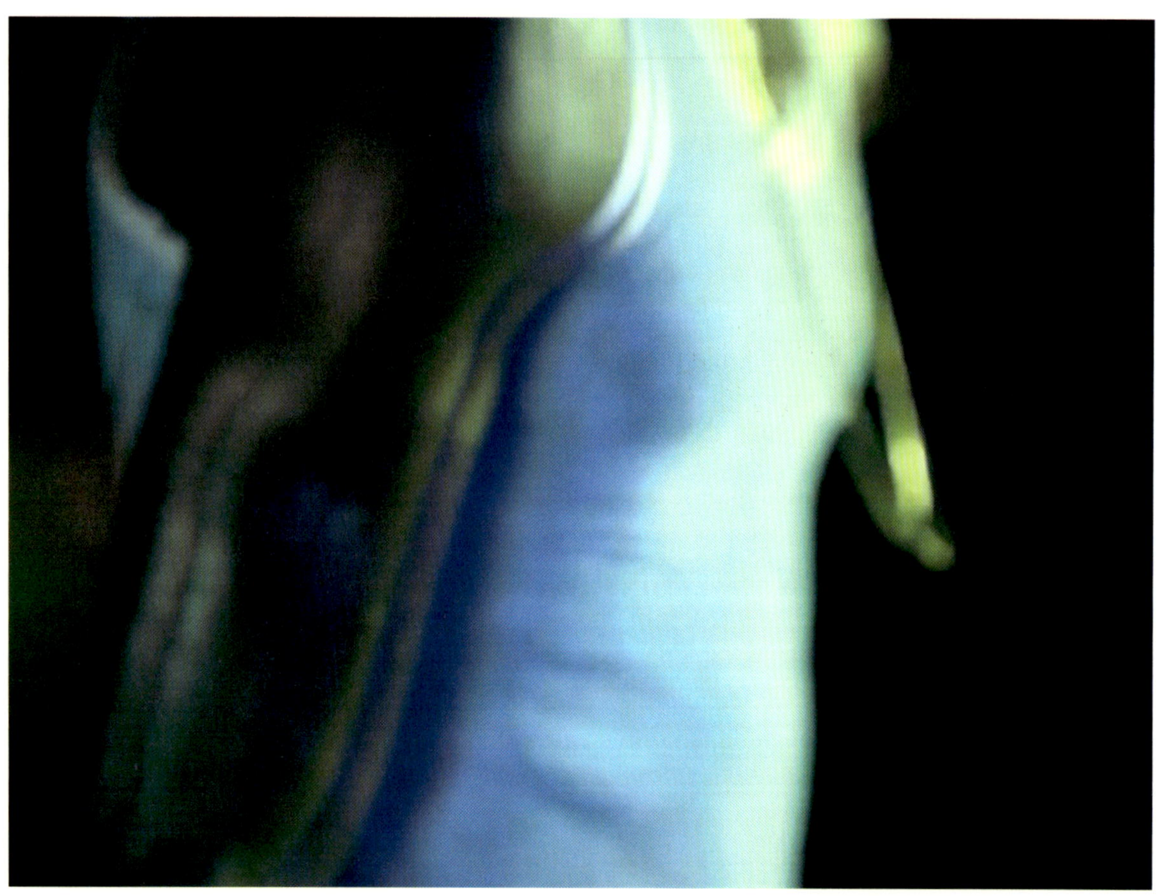

Sable Elyse Smith, *Men Who Swallow Themselves in Mirrors*, 2017 (stills)

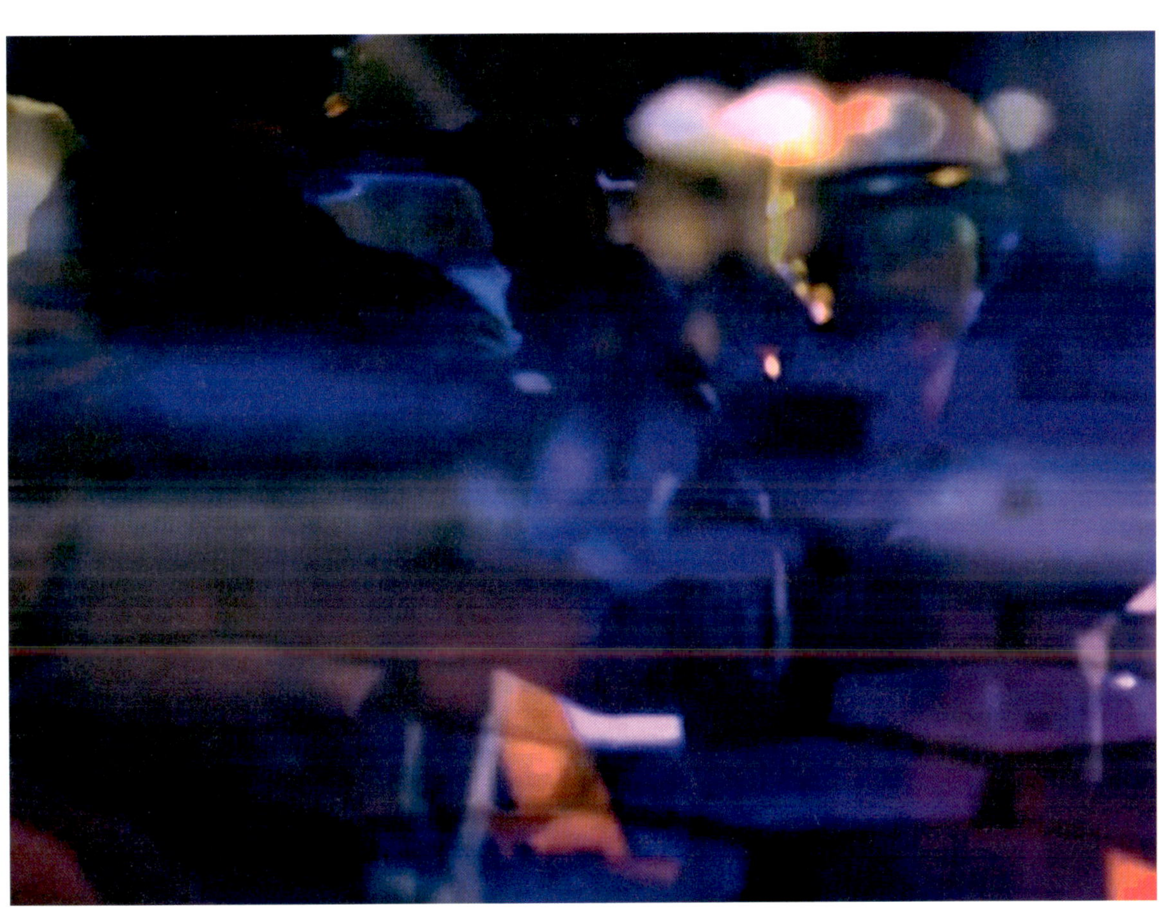

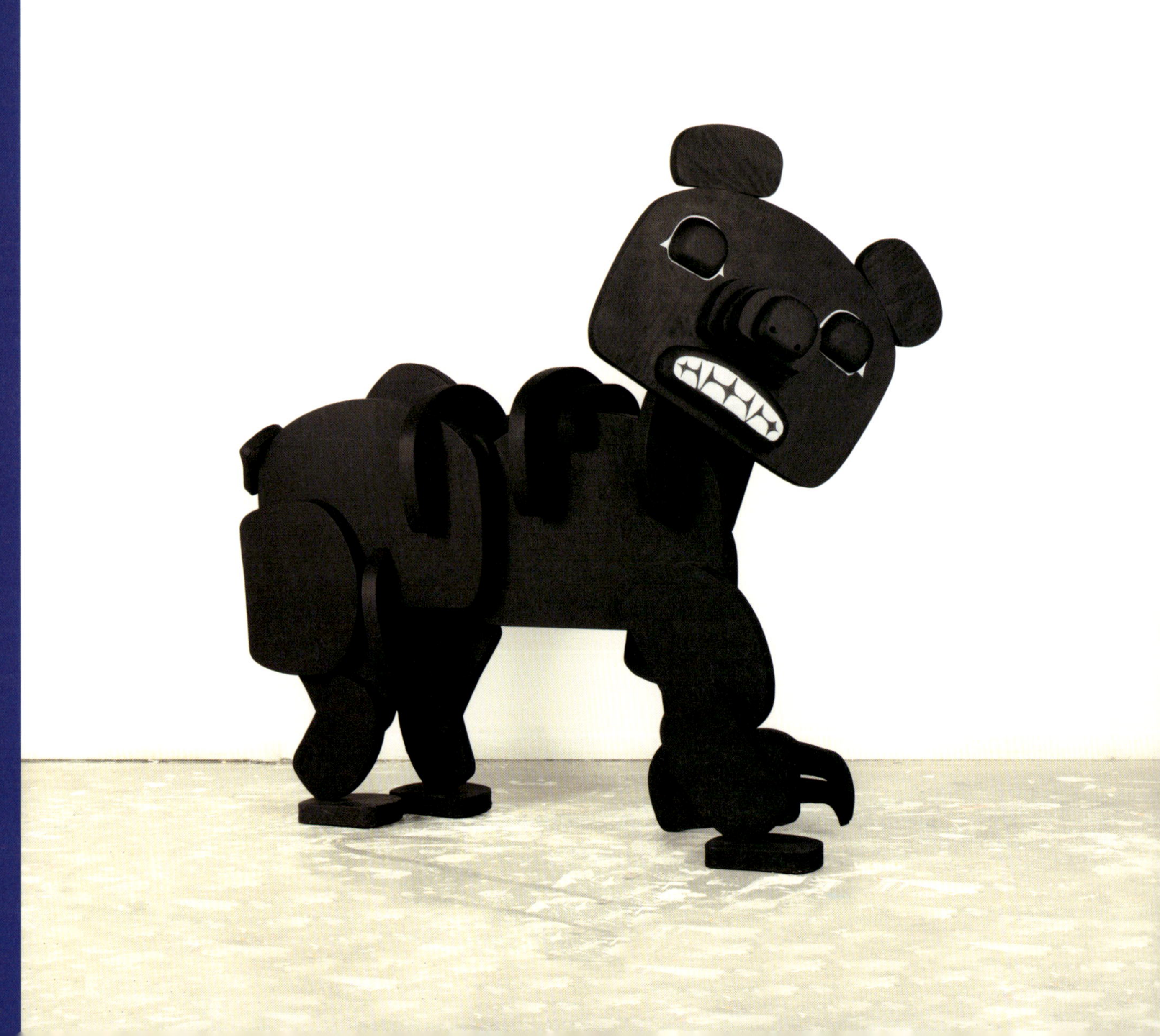

# WORKS IN THE EXHIBITION

Unless otherwise indicated, artworks are courtesy
of the artists.

**Lutz Bacher**
(b. 1943 in Berkeley, USA; lives in New York)

*Rocket*, 2016–18
Color photograph printed on vinyl
10 x 40 feet (3 x 12.1 m)
Courtesy of the artist and Greene Naftali, New York
† SITE Santa Fe commission

*Whiteboard*, 2018
Whiteboard, marker
48 x 96 inches (121.9 x 243.8 cm)
Courtesy of the artist and Greene Naftali, New York

*Open the Kimono*, 2018
Digital slideshow
Duration variable
Courtesy of the artist and Greene Naftali, New York


**Ángela Bonadies**
(b. 1970 in Caracas; lives in Madrid, ESP, and Caracas)
and
**Juan José Olavarría**
(b. 1969 in Valencia, VEN; lives in Buenos Aires, ARG)

*La Torre de David*, 2010–ongoing
Digital prints, drawing
Varying dimensions

**Melissa Cody**
(b. 1983 in No Water Mesa, USA; lives in Los Angeles)

*US*, 2015
Wool, aniline dyes
34 ½ x 13 inches (87.6 x 33 cm)
Collection of Malia Sias

*Sweet lovable . . . You*, 2016
Wool, aniline dyes
27 x 43 ½ inches (68.5 x 110.5 cm)
Collection of Alain and David Macklovitch

*Home*, 2016
Wool, aniline dyes
Approx. 24 x 16 inches (61 x 40.6 cm)
Collection of Adam Gianotti

*Dreamscape*, 2016
Wool, aniline dyes
Approx. 18 x 13 inches (45.7 x 33 cm)
Collection of Joshua Rose

*Water's Edge*, 2016
Wool, aniline dyes
26 ½ x 15 ½ inches (67.3 x 39.3 cm)
Collection of Franci Neely

*4th Dimension*, 2016
Wool, aniline dyes
26 ½ x 15 ½ inches (67.3 x 39.3 cm)
Collection of Samuel La Fountain

Lawerence Paul Yuxweluptun, *Black Bear*, 2018

*Woven in the Stones*, 2018
Wool, aniline dyes
28 x 38 inches (71.1 x 96.5 cm)
† SITE Santa Fe commission

## Paz Errázuriz
(b. 1944 Santiago, CHL; lives in Santiago)

From the series
*Nómadas del mar* (Nomads of the sea), 1996
Digital prints of analog photographs
Each 19 ⅝ x 23 ⅝ inches (50 x 60 cm)

From the series
*Niñas* (Girls), 2018
Made with contributions by Sergio Parra
Digital prints of analog photographs paired with ID
cards issued by the Chilean police to track and survey
sex workers in the city of Talca, Chile, between 1968
and 1976
16 ⅞ x 12 ⅝ inches (43 x 32 cm)
Courtesy of the artist and Sergio Parra
† SITE Santa Fe commission

## Victor Estrada
(b. 1956 in Los Angeles, USA; lives in Los Angeles)

*Pink Cloud / Chocolate Mountain / Blue Sky with
Shadow*, 2017
Oil on canvas over panel
24 x 18 inches (61 x 45.7 cm)
Courtesy of the artist and Richard Telles Fine Art, Los Angeles

*The Spirit of the Living and the Dead and Cotton
Candy / Posada*, 2017
Oil on panel
48 x 60 inches (121.9 x 152.4 cm)
Courtesy of the artist and Richard Telles Fine Art, Los Angeles

*I Went Walking and She Threw Me a Look / aka
"Froggie Went a Courtin"*, 2017
Oil on canvas over panel
48 x 60 inches (121.9 x 152.4 cm)
Courtesy of the artist and Richard Telles Fine Art, Los Angeles

## Andrea Fraser
(b. 1965 in Billings, USA; lives in Los Angeles)

*2016 in Museums, Money, and Politics*, 2018
Vinyl
Dimensions variable
† SITE Santa Fe commission

## Hock E Aye Vi Edgar Heap of Birds
(b. 1954 in Wichita, USA; lives in Oklahoma City)

*Surviving Active Shooter Custer*, 2018
Monoprints and ghost prints on buff rag paper
48 prints, each 22 x 30 inches (55.8 x 76.2 cm)
† SITE Santa Fe commission

## Fernanda Laguna
(b. 1972 in Buenos Aires, ARG; lives in Buenos Aires)

*Pintada, no vacía pintada está mi casa*
(Painted, not void/my house is painted), 2018
Installation: various materials, including the following paintings:

*Mi yo escondido I* (My hidden self I), 2017
Acrylic on canvas, collage
24 ⅜ x 12 ⅞ inches (62 x 33 cm)

*Mi yo escondido II* (My hidden self II), 2017
Acrylic on canvas and collage
24 ⅜ x 12 ⅞ inches (62 x 33 cm)

*Mi yo escondido III* (My hidden self III), 2017
Acrylic on canvas and collage
19 ⅝ x 12 ⅞ inches (50 x 33 cm)

*Te quiero mucho* (I love you so much), 2017
Acrylic on canvas and collage
15 ⅜ x 13 ¾ inches (39 x 35 cm)

*Untitled*, 2017
Acrylic on canvas and collage
19 ⅝ x 13 inches (50 x 33 cm)

*Untitled*, 2017
Acrylic on canvas with cutouts
26 ¼ x 24 4/10 inches (67 x 62 cm)

*Untitled*, 2017
Acrylic on canvas and collage
24 ⅖ x 20 ⅜ inches (62 x 52 cm)

All courtesy of the artist and Galería Nora Fisch, Buenos Aires
† SITE Santa Fe commission


**Victoria Mamnguqsualuk**
(b. 1930 near Hanningajuq, Nunavut; d. 2016 in
Baker Lake, Nunavut)

*Untitled*, 1981
Wall hanging, wool felt, embroidery thread on wool duffel
47 ⅜ x 49 ⅝ inches (120.5 x 126 cm)
Courtesy of Government of Nunavut Fine Art Collection
and the Winnipeg Art Gallery

*Untitled*, 1980
Wall hanging, wool felt, embroidery thread on wool duffel
31 ½ x 28 ¾ inches (80 x 73 cm)
Courtesy of Government of Nunavut Fine Art Collection
and the Winnipeg Art Gallery

*Untitled*, 1983
Colored pencil on black paper
22 x 30 inches (56 x 76.5 cm)
Courtesy of Government of Nunavut Fine Art Collection
Collection and the Winnipeg Art Gallery

*Untitled*, 1982
Colored pencil on black paper
30 x 44 inches (76.5 x112.2 cm)
Courtesy of Government of Nunavut Fine Art Collection
Collection and the Winnipeg Art Gallery

*Legend*, 1993
Colored pencil on paper
22 x 30 inches (55.8 x 76.2 cm)
Courtesy of Feheley Fine Arts

*Catching the Fish Mother*, 1979
Linocut and stencil on paper
24 ½ x 33 inches (62.2 x 84 cm)
Courtesy of Feheley Fine Arts

*Camping Scene with Father Holding Sting of Fish*, early 2000s
Colored pencil and graphite on paper
22 ¼ x 30 inches (61.5 x 76.2 cm)
Courtesy of Feheley Fine Arts

*Two Teams Compete to Play the String Game*, 2006
Stencil on paper
24 ½ x 39 inches (62.2 x 99 cm)
Courtesy of Feheley Fine Arts

*Snake Man*, 1982
Stonecut and stencil print
30 x 37 inches (76.2 x 94 cm)
Private collection

*Flesh-Eating Monster*, 1984
Stonecut and stencil print
33 ½ x 25 inches (85.1 x 63.5 cm)
Private collection

*Inside the Iglu*, 1987
Stonecut and stencil print
37 ½ x 26 inches (95.3 x 66 cm)
Private collection

*Conversing with the Snake Spirit*, 1987
Woodcut and stencil print
38 x 26 inches (96.5 x 66 cm)
Private collection

*Underwater Creatures*, 1988
26 x 19 inches (66 x 48.3 cm)
Stonecut and stencil print
Private collection

**Jumana Manna**
(b. 1987 in Princeton, USA; lives in Berlin, DEU, and Beirut, LBN)

*Wild Relatives*, 2018
HD video (color, sound; 66:00 minutes)

**Eduardo Navarro**
(b. 1979 in Buenos Aries, ARG; lives in Buenos Aires)

*Galactic Playground*, 2018
Concrete, paint, text, sunlight
Diameter: 32 feet (9.8 m)
† SITE Santa Fe commission
Special thanks to the Santa Fe Railyard Art Projects

**NuMu**
(El Nuevo Museo de Arte Contemporáneo) (est. 2012 in
Guatemala City, GTM, by Stefan Benchoam and Jessica Kairé)

Traveling 1:1 replica of artist-run space in Guatemala
Fiberglass
7 ¾ x 8 ¾ feet (2.4 x 2.7 m)
Courtesy of Stefan Benchoam and Jessica Kairé

On view at NuMu, within *Casa tomada*,
August–October 2018:

Radamés "Juni" Figueroa
*El nido salvaje* (The wild nest), 2013/2018
Courtesy of the artist and NuMu

On view at NuMu, within *Casa tomada*,
November 2018–January 2019:

To be announced
† SITE Santa Fe commission

**Tania Pérez Córdova**
(b. 1979 in Mexico City, MEX; lives in Mexico City)

*A man flexing his muscle to show off his strength*, 2017
Petrified earth dried in the shade
2 ¾ x 11 ⅜ x 8 ¾ inches (7 x 29 x 22 cm)
Courtesy of the artist and José Garcia, Mexico

*Blink*, 2017
Marble, blue cosmetic right-eye contact lens (left-eye
contact worn by someone)
Height: 32 inches (81.3 cm); diameter: 4 ¾ inches (12.4 cm)
Courtesy of the artist and José Garcia, Mexico

*Placebo*, 2017
Aluminum cast of a hole in a hill, nine fake gold neck-
laces, one real gold necklace
Dimensions variable
Courtesy of the artist and José Garcia, Mexico

*Time-lapse*, 2017
Petrified earth dried in the shade, makeup, cigarette butt,
plastic wrapping, Mexican 50-peso note
39 x 25 ½ x 1 inch (99.1x 69.9 x 2.9 cm)
Courtesy of the artist and José Garcia, Mexico

*Portrait of a Woman Unknown 1*, 2018
Oil on wood, occasionally a woman wearing a dress
Dimensions variable
† SITE Santa Fe commission

*Portrait of a Woman Unknown 2*, 2018
Oil on wood, occasionally a woman wearing a dress
Dimensions variable
† SITE Santa Fe commission

## Jamasee Pitseolak
(b. 1968 in Cape Dorset, CAN; lives in Cape Dorset)

*Lady*, 2011
Stone
4 ½ x 6 x 2 ½ inches (11.4 x 15.2 x 6.3 cm)
Collection of Marnie Schreiber
Courtesy of Marion Scott Gallery, Vancouver

*Peter Pitseolak's Chair*, 2009
Stone, string, caribou antler
5 x 3 ¼ x 3 ¼ inches (12.7 x 8.2 x 8.2 cm)
Collection of Marnie Schreiber
Courtesy of Marion Scott Gallery, Vancouver

*Laden Sole*, 2004
Stone
4 ½ x 8 x 1 ¾ inches (11.4 x 20.3 x 4.4 cm)
Courtesy of Marion Scott Gallery, Vancouver

*Toe-Nailed*, 2006
Stone, musk ox horn, caribou antler
3 x 3 ½ x 3 inches (7.6 x 8.8 x 7.6 cm)
Courtesy of Marion Scott Gallery, Vancouver

*Musk Ox Pistol*, 2011
Stone, msuk ox horn
10 ¾ x 5 ½ x 2 inches (27.3 x 13.9 x 5 cm)
Collection of John and Joyce Price
Courtesy of Marion Scott Gallery, Vancouver

*Domestic Sewing Machine*, 2006
Stone, ivory
4 ½ x 6 x 2 ½ inches (11.4 x 15.2 x 6.3 cm)
Collection of John and Joyce Price
Courtesy of Marion Scott Gallery, Vancouver

*Grandpa's Corner*, 2006
Stone
Table: 2 ⅞ x 2 ¾ x 2 ⅜ inches (7.4 x 7 x 6 cm)
Chair: 4 ¼ x 1 ½ x 1 ¾ inches (11 x 3.8 x 4.6 cm)
Radio: 1 ⅛ x 1 ¾ x ½ inches (2.7 x 4.5 x 1.4 cm)
Collection of John and Joyce Price
Courtesy of Marion Scott Gallery, Vancouver

## Naufus Ramírez-Figueroa
(b. 1978 in Guatemala City, GTM; lives in Berlin,
DEU, and Guatemala City)

*Revindication of Tangible Property*, 2018
Sculptural installation: wood, expanded
polystyrene, epoxy resin, mineral pigments
Dimenssions variable
Courtesy of the artist and Proyectos Ultravioleta,
Guatemala City; Mendes Wood DM, São Paulo;
and Sies & Höke, Düsseldorf
† SITE Santa Fe commission

## Eric-Paul Riege
(b. 1994 in Gallup, USA; lives in Gallup)

*diyin+, hooghan and weaving dance (fig.3) for
Na'ashjéíí Asdzáá, Retha, Effie, and Angela*, 2018
Mixed-media installation, digital print on paper, performance
† SITE Santa Fe commission

**Curtis Talwst Santiago**
(b. 1979 in Toronto, CAN; lives in Lisbon, PRT)

From *Infinity Series*, 2008–ongoing
Mixed media dioramas in reclaimed jewelry boxes
Varying dimensions
Courtesy of the artist; Rachel Uffner Gallery,
New York; and private collections

**Sable Elyse Smith**
(b. 1986 in Los Angeles, USA; lives in New York)

*Landscape IV*, 2018
22 x 120 x 4 inches (56 x 305 x 10 cm)
Courtesy of the artist and JTT, New York
† SITE Santa Fe commission

*Men Who Swallow Themselves in Mirrors*, 2017
Single-channel video (color, sound; 8:32 minutes)
Courtesy of the artist and JTT, New York

## Stephanie Taylor

(b. 1971 in New York, USA; lives in Los Angeles)

*Press Release Songs*, 2017–18
Songs announcing *SITElines.2018: Casa tomada*
Vocals: Monika Beal, Josh Bedlion, Natalie Clegg, Sean
Fitzpatrick, Baraka May
Trombone: Michael Vlatkovich
Arrangement: Casey Butler
Transcription: Baraka May
Engineer: Jake Viator
† SITE Santa Fe commission

*Miraculous Fermentations*, 2018
Photographic-still video (color, sound; 9:53 minutes)
Vocals: Monika Bealm, Josh Bedlion, Monika Bruckner,
Natalie Clegg, Sean Fitzpatrick, Andreas Preponis,
Nani Sinha
Wagner tuba: Steve Durbin
Engineer: Jake Viator
Transcription: Baraka May
Text from Thomas Mann, *The Transposed Heads: A Legend of
India* (1941), Jonathan Gold, *Counter Intelligence: Where to
Eat in the Real Los Angeles* (2000)
† SITE Santa Fe commission

Made possible with generous support from Villa Aurora
and Thomas Mann House e. V.

## Lawrence Paul Yuxweulptun

(b. 1957 in Kamloops, CAN; lives in Vancouver)

*Floor Opener*, 2013
Acrylic on canvas
76 x 96 inches (193 x 244 cm)
Collection of Inna and Michael O'Brian

*Neo Totems*, 2018
Acrylic paint, cedar
Five sculptures, varying dimensions
Courtesy of the artist and Macaulay & Co. Fine Art
† SITE Santa Fe commission

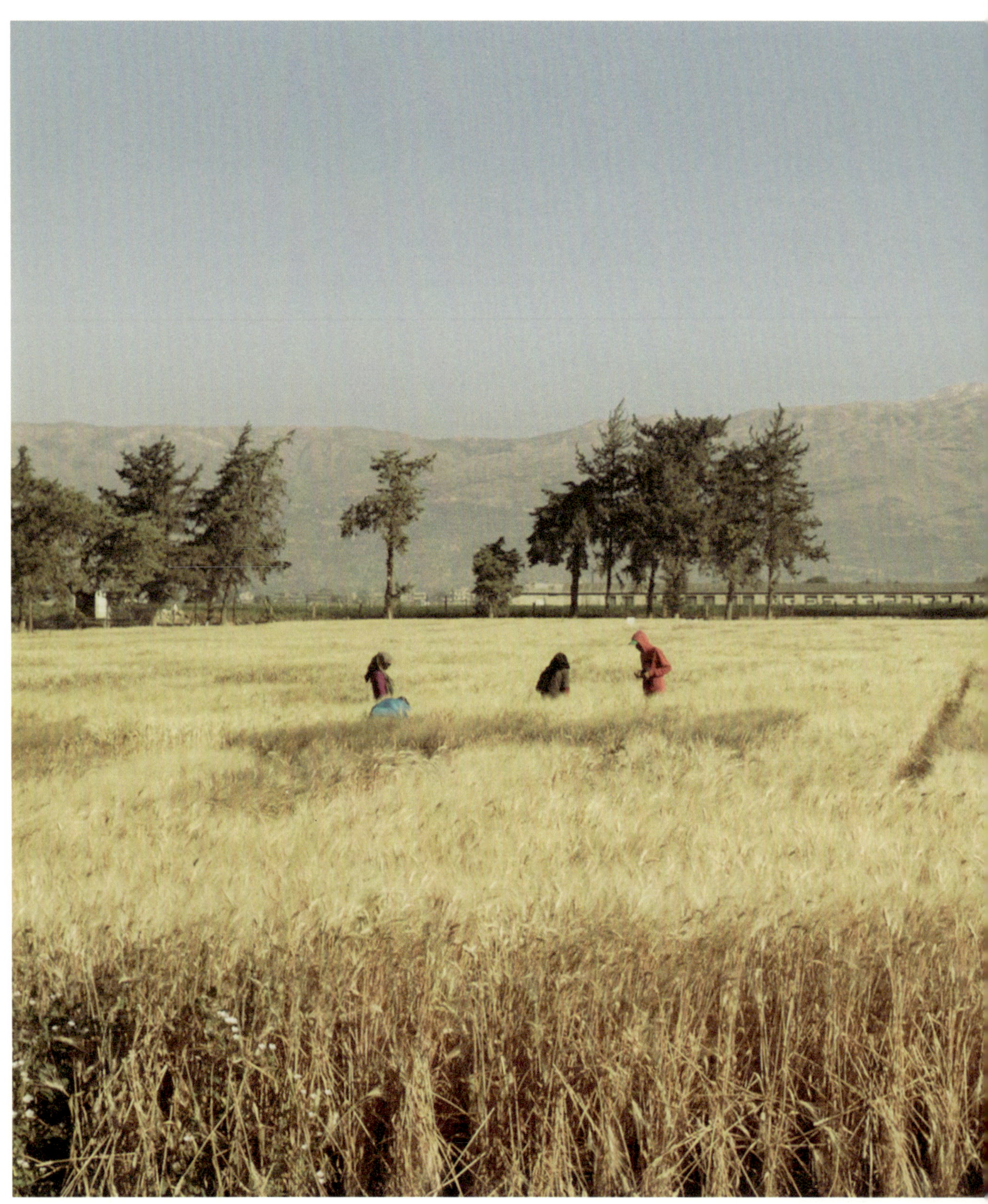

Jumana Manna, *Wild Relatives*, 2018 (still)

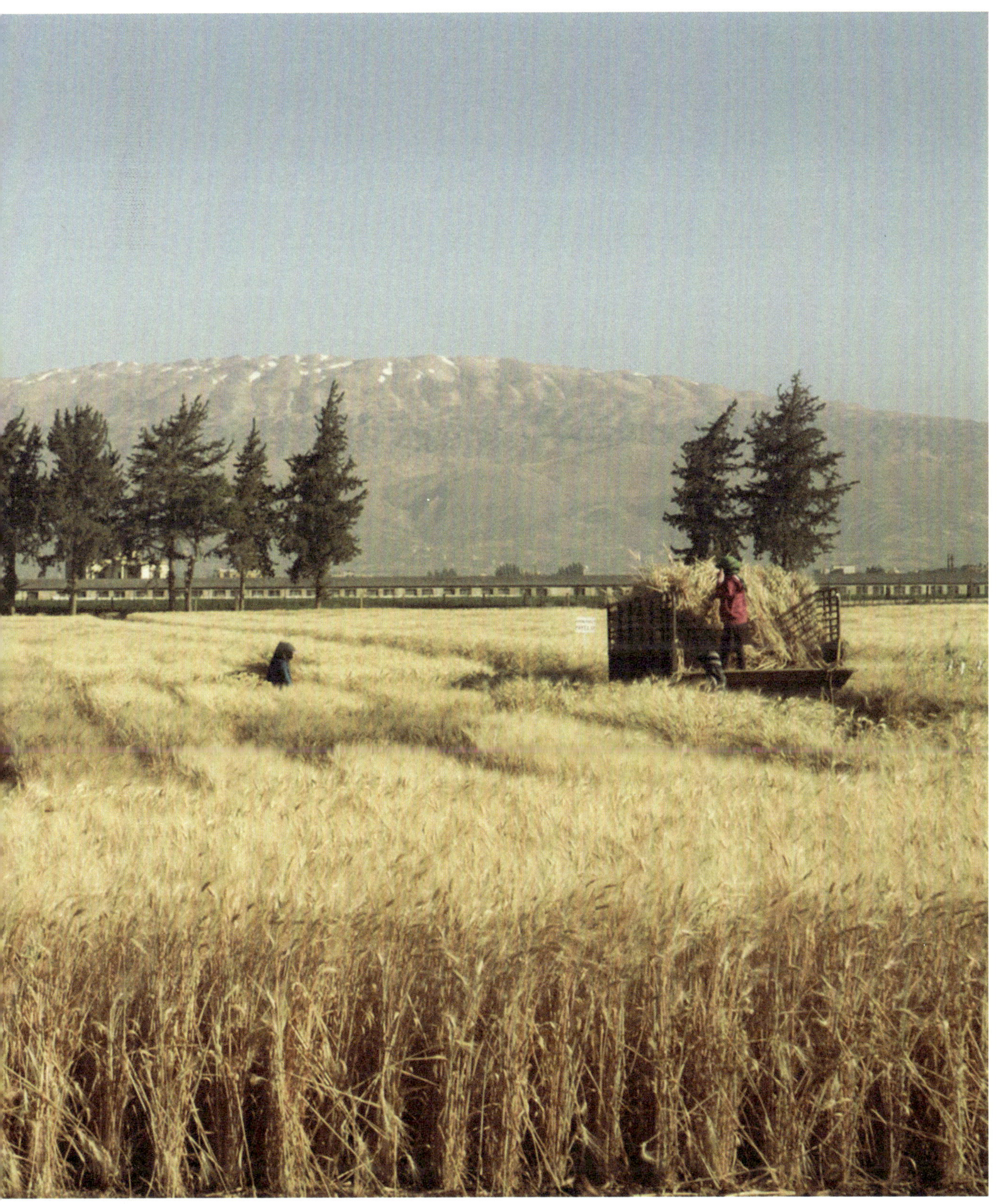

# SCALP, TEA, HORSE, VASE, BANANA, STICK
### Magalí Arriola

Here is a hypothetical scene: Two siblings live in their old family house. This could be in the province of Buenos Aires, most likely in the year 1946, though it could be before or at a much later date. Furniture, objects, murmurs, and sounds begin to move from the role of incidental props and atmospheric details to that of directors of the staging and plot of the story.

And here is a parallel conjecture: Props that have been instrumentalized to tell one version of a story resurface as the remnants of historical fact that offer a very different version of that same story, deconstructing rituals and myths to, ultimately, elicit new forms of exchange and communication.

*The Backstory: The Princess of Wales Riding in a Coach*

5th Avenue Hotel, New York,
June 29th, 1887.

HON. WM. F. CODY,
London, England.

DEAR CODY,—. . . . . . . .

. . . . . . . In common with all your countrymen, I want to let you know that I am not only gratified, but proud of your management and general behavior; so far as I can make out you have been modest, graceful, and dignified in all you have done to illustrate the history of civilization on this Continent during the past century.

I am especially pleased with the graceful and pretty compliment paid to you by the Princess of Wales, who rode in the Deadwood Coach while it was attacked by the Indians, and rescued by the Cowboys. Such things did occur in our days, and may never again.

As near as I can estimate there were *in* 1865 *about nine and a half of millions of buffaloes* on the plains between the Missouri River and the Rocky Mountains, all are now gone—killed for their meat, their skins and bones.

This seems like desecration, cruelty, and murder, yet they have been replaced by twice as many *neat* cattle. At that date there were about 165,000 *Pawnees, Sioux, Cheyennes, Kiowas, and Arapahoes,* who depended on these buffaloes for their yearly food. They, too, are gone, and have been replaced by twice or thrice as many white men and women, who have made the earth to blossom as the rose, and who can be counted, taxed, and governed by the laws of nature and civilization. This change has been salutary, and will go on to the end. You have caught one epoch of the world's history; have illustrated it in the very heart of the modern world—London, and I want you to feel that on this side of the water we appreciate it.

This drama must end; days, years and centuries follow fast, even the drama of civilization must have an end. . . .

Sincerely your friend,
W. T. SHERMAN.
WAR DEPARTMENT, ADJUTANT-GENERAL'S OFFICE, WASHINGTON, August 10, 1886.[1]


What William Tecumseh Sherman didn't foresee is that what he saw as the close of the "drama of civilization" was actually the starting point of a cultural and political confrontation that would gain complexity over time as diverse cultures and nations—not only from the East and West, but also from the North and South—perceived one another as ungraspable reflections. Nor could Sherman predict that the spectacle that William

F. Cody launched in Nebraska in 1883 as Buffalo Bill's Wild West, a cover-up for what Sherman himself describes as the settlers' "desecration, cruelty, and murder" intended to provoke a frisson of self-satisfied excitement in the colonial mind, would decline only with Cody's bankruptcy in 1913.[2]

Nicknamed Buffalo Bill for allegedly having killed 4,282 buffalo (essential to Plains populations, as Sherman notes) in eighteen months, Cody was an American scout for the US Army who constructed for himself a dubious reputation not only as a bison hunter but also a Pony Express rider, protagonist of fiction, and, most memorably, a showman. Buffalo Bill's Wild West quickly evolved into an outdoor event purporting to recreate the experience of being on the Great Plains. Its open-air stage was filled with actors in cowboy outfits, Native Americans playing themselves, buffalo and horses doing tricks, musicians, and cheering crowds. Despite the entertainment value of the show, the management of Buffalo Bill's Wild West made a point of identifying it not as a spectacle but as a "locale" for historical tableaux. The organizers intended "to do more than present an exacting and realistic entertainment for public amusement. The object [was] to picture TO THE EYE, by the aid of historical characters and living animals, a series of animated scenes and episodes."[3] The authenticity of the events was supposedly based on Buffalo Bill's experience as a frontiersman. However, these reenactments were "not recreations, but reductions of complex events into 'typical scenes,' based on the formulas of popular literary mythology. . . . If the Wild West was a place rather than a show, then its landscape was a mythic space, in which past and present, fiction and reality could co-exist; a space in which history, translated into myth, was reenacted as ritual."[4] The organizers never acknowledged the fact that the representation of this mythology relied on its performance by figures who actually participated in historical events, such as Sitting Bull and Geronimo, who, having been incarcerated, found their way out of prison only by agreeing to play themselves in a rewritten and denigrating script.

These revisionist narratives had to be ritualistically repeated in order to legitimize the continental expansion of European-descended populations known as Manifest Destiny, which justified the takeover of what historian Frederick Jackson Turner in 1893 called "an area of free land." In a famous address to the American Historical Association, Turner wrote about the vigorous spirit and dominant individualism—the "American intellect"—that developed out of the exploration of the frontier. It was, he maintained, closely tied to the development of commerce and the providential unfolding of liberty and self-governance. From such a perspective, force was seen as a redemptive and restorative duty, exerted to the detriment of other cultures to promote (self-advantageously conceived) concepts of law, justice, and democracy. A few armed men took upon themselves the responsibility of establishing their own notion of law and order, while evading justice themselves.[5]

*Intermission:* Horses Don't Lie[6]

*When in the distance you see a herd of creatures that are neither fully equine nor fully human. Horse-costumed performers bearing wooden prostheses project an image of trust between human and animals, their mutual confidence achieved by touch therapy, an approach that bypasses language to discover new modes of communication.*

A 1901 review in the *New York Times* described Buffalo Bill's Wild West as a "series of pictures."[7] Popular scenes or tableaux presented pictures of the settlement of the Great Plains, life on the cattle ranch, the buffalo hunt, and the attacks on the Deadwood Stage Coach, interspersed with displays of cowboy fun, trick riding, and roping. But the program also included a brutal scene in which Cody scalped a young warrior called Yellow Hair to avenge what he saw as General George Custer's disastrous defeat at Little Bighorn. The real Yellow Hair's scalp was one of the props used to lend verisimilitude, framing Custer's downfall as irrefutable proof of the savageness and brutality of the Native populations, his own genocidal aggressions ignored as a cause of their decimation and subjugation.

For Richard Slotkin, "the Wild West's evolution from a memorialization of the past to a celebration of the imperial future" is marked by a pivotal change Cody made in the program: "The Wild West's conflation of the Frontier Myth and the new ideology of imperialism was fully achieved in 1899 when 'Custer's Last Fight' was replaced by the 'Battle of San Juan Hill' that celebrated the heroism of Theodore Roosevelt—whose First Volunteers Cavalry Regiment was best known by its nickname 'The Rough Riders' [the name taken from Cody's spectacle]."[8] The Battle of San Juan Hill, waged the year before in Cuba by the First US Volunteer Cavalry under the command of then-Colonel Roosevelt, marked the end of the Spanish-American War, after which the US took over the territory of Guantánamo in Cuba and received the Philippines from Spain as part of

war reparations. Soon sworn into office as the twenty-sixth US president, in 1901, Roosevelt was fond of quoting the purportedly African saying "Speak softly and carry a big stick" to serve as a prop for supporting foreign policy whose coerciveness had an impact well beyond his administration. Having drafted a corollary to the Monroe Doctrine that stated that the US would use military force against any "wrongdoing" that might destabilize the continent, Roosevelt hoped thereby to dissuade European powers from intervening in the Americas, an argument that was used repeatedly by later presidents to justify North American interventions in countries like Chile, Guatemala, Haiti, and Nicaragua.[9]

*Intermission:* Bananas Ripening to the Weight of Your Sweet Love[10]

*When a bunch of bananas turns yellow, with the warm embrace of a body as the ultimate expression of reparations for political malfeasance; when bananas grow limbs, and bodies grow bananas; when naming comes to symbolize the taming of nature and the colonization of the social body—a personal, stagelike narrative is told in which objects amend history.*

*Nine Lakota Drinking Tea*

During that same period, in 1898 there was "a studio tea up town . . . which probably exceeded in originality anything in the nature of an entertainment of that kind ever given. . . . The studio—*The New York Times* reported—was that of Mrs. Gertrude Käsebier and the gentlemen present were, among others, Mr. High Heron. Mr. Has No Horses, Mr. Sammy Lone Bear, Mr. Shooting Pieces, Mr. Iron Tail, and Mr. Red Horn Bull. They were nine Sioux Indians, and they were taking tea with Mrs. Käsebier by special request, for the sake of *auld land syne*."[11] Though the author of the *New York Times* article implies that photographer Gertrude Käsebier's gesture was a nostalgic farewell to the bygone years of the frontier, it is more likely that she brought her vision to a more knowing ambition—to document a moment of transition from the conditions of a recent past to those of an emerging future in which, according to the imperial impulse, progress was understood to naturally require invasion and violation of the landscape and its inhabitants. In the words of W. J. T. Mitchell, "empires move outward in space as a way of moving forward in time; the prospect that opens up is not just a spatial scene but a projected future of development and exploitation."[12]

Best known for intimate motherhood scenes, Käsebier was closely associated with Alfred Stieglitz's circle. Having grown up on the Big Plains of the Colorado Territories, she was familiar with Native populations. After Buffalo Bill's Wild West troupe paraded past her studio windows on Fifth Avenue to announce a three-week run at Madison Square Garden, she wrote Cody asking to invite over some of the performers who had chosen to leave the Pine Ridge Agency reservation in South Dakota to join his company. The result was the establishment of relationships maintained for over a dozen years, as well as a seductive series of photographic portraits whose problematic raises a number of questions about issues of representation and identity.

Federal rules forbade Native populations from wearing their regalia and performing traditional ceremonies on the reservations, but within the bare walls of Käsebier's studio the Lakota visitors could wear their own clothes. In this isolated environment, they could do so without overstating their cultural identity in the theatricalized way required of them when performing their scripted supporting roles in front of a crowd. Over time, Käsebier suggested the possibility of their setting aside their traditional attire to assume what, from her vantage point, would be a more neutral manner of self-presentation, as individuals rather than as tribal members habitually misinterpreted by white viewers. She intuited that the privacy of the studio would encourage her sitters to unwind, to socialize, smoke cigarettes, and make drawings. Collectively and individually, they made representations of bison, spotted horses, cowboys, and their own people that she mounted on sheets of paper underneath the portraits she made. Her archive also holds letters they wrote her and their personal account of their victory over Custer—the mirrored version of the invented story of defeat they were hired to repeatedly perform. The account is framed with sketches of tipis, arrows, quivers, and shields, not props but instrumental elements for what turned out to be one of the Lakota people's last triumphs, one that was turned against them by Cody's spectacle.

*Intermission:* Dogs When Barking (They Say)[13]

*When objects narrate a new version of the history of a place, in the manner of archaeological finds, inside and outside the exhibition space: the windowpanes of an artist studio facing north, a cigarette butt left behind, a glass vase, the missing foot of an equestrian sculpture.*

In her studio, Käsebier created a space removed from distorting theatrical settings, and, to a certain extent, imposed less impediment or mediation than was usually practiced in such endeavors. The photographer—in this case, a white female artist—and models synthesized complicity and sociability, images and storytelling (in both sketches and photographs), effecting an exchange of gazes that, from today's perspective, appears to embody an experiment in the cross-cultural "drama of civilization" that was starting to take shape—that of the conflicting voices and interpretations of Indigenous cultures and their colonizers. This drama continues to this day in a variety of forms all over the globe.

*Last Act:* Most Serene Republics[14]

*When a blown-glass vessel seems to contain the soaring spirits of those who died under coercion and constraint; when their bonds to a territory stand not as a gesture for colonization but as a renewed and peaceful connection with the land.*

ENDNOTES

1. Letter from W. T. Sherman to W. F. Cody, June 29, 1887, William F. Cody Archive: Documenting the Life and Times of Buffalo Bill website, http://codyarchive.org/memorabilia/wfc.mem00277.html.

2. In the early 1990s, Cody's spectacle would be revived as "Buffalo Bill's Wild West Show with Mickey and His Friends" at EuroDisney, Paris, which endures to this day. Except for the actors, there have been no changes in the presentation.

3. "Salutatory," Buffalo Bill's Wild West program, 1886, quoted in Richard Slotkin, "Buffalo Bill's 'Wild West' and the Mythologization of the American Empire," *Cultures of United States Imperialism*, ed. Amy Kaplan and Donald E. Pease (Durham, NC: Duke University Press, 1993), 165.

4. Ibid., 166.

5. Turner's speech was first presented during the Chicago Columbian Exhibition organized to commemorate the four-hundredth anniversary of the "discovery" of the Americas, one of a series of international expositions embodying the spectacularization of colonial experience. Frederick Jackson Turner, "The Significance of the Frontier in American History," 1893, American Historical Society website, https://www.historians.org/about-aha-and-membership/aha-history-and-archives/historical-archives/the-significance-of-the-frontier-in-american-history.

6. Eduardo Navarro, *Horses Don't Lie*, 2013, performance, presented during the 9th Mercosul Biennial, Porto Alegre, Brazil (2013).

7. "Indians in the Wild West Show: Even When Not Performing They Wear Native Dress," *New York Times*, April 21, 1901, quoted in Michelle Delaney, *Buffalo Bill's Wild West Warriors: A Photographic Study by Gertrude Käsebier* (Washington, DC: Smithsonian Institution), 33.

8. Slotkin, "'Buffalo Bill's 'Wild West' and the Mythologization of the American Empire," 175–76. The press nicknamed Roosevelt's regiment the "Rough Riders" after Cody's show, whose name had been changed in 1893 to "Buffalo Bill's Wild West and Congress of Rough Riders of the World" to refer to the incorporation of skilled horsemen from various countries.

9. Roosevelt drafted the corollary in 1904, with construction of the Panama Canal in mind. See United States History website, http://www.u-s-history.com/pages/h1449.html.

10. Naufus Ramírez-Figueroa, *Bananas Ripening to the Weight of Your Sweet Love*, 2008, performance.

11. Elizabeth Hutchinson, "When the 'Sioux Party Chief Calls': Käsebier's Indian Portraits and the Gendering of the Artist's Studio," *American Art* 16, no. 2 (Summer 2002), 40–65, available through JSTOR at https://www.academia.edu/23409262/When_the_Sioux_Chiefs_Party_Calls_Käsebiers_Indian_Portraits_and_the_Gendering_of_the_Artists_Studio. The New York Times article Hutchinson cites is dated April 10, 1898. Other historians, like Delaney, cite April 24, 1898, as the day the Sioux first came to Käsebier's studio, which appears to be correct. See Delaney, *Buffalo Bill's Wild West Warriors*, 13.

12. W. J. T. Mitchell, "Imperial Landscape," in *Landscape and Power*, ed. W. J. T. Mitchell (Chicago: University of Chicago Press, 1993), 17.

13. Tania Pérez Córdova, *Dogs When Barking (They Say)*, 2015, window glazing, adhesive plastic, and cigarette butt, 18 ½ x 34 ⅝ x 7 ⅞ in. (47 x 87.9 x 20 cm). Courtesy José García.

14. Hock E Aye Vi Edgar Heap of Birds, *Most Serene Republic: Native Bodies of Remembrance*, 2007. The abstract forms on these blown-glass vases, reminiscent of the artist's *Neuf* paintings, constitute an homage to those who perished as victims of accidents and diseases during Cody's European tours and whose bodies were never repatriated to their own land. For an analysis of the *Neuf* paintings' relation to land as a dynamic and all-embracing entity—as opposed to the European concept of land as property—see Jean Fisher, "Remembering the Future: Traditional and Modernity in the work of Hock E Aye Vi Edgar Heap of Birds," Jean Fisher website, http://www.jeanfisher.com/remembering-the-future-tradition-and-modernity-in-the-work-of-hock-e-aye-vi-edgar-heap-of-birds/.

# DISPOSSESSION

Evan Calder Williams

*Comfort is paradoxically produced by two seemingly opposing conditions, intimacy and control.*

–Beatriz Colomina

*But you cannot build a house out of carpets.*

–Adolf Loos

### Heat, cold, rain, thieves, and the inquisitive

In Le Corbusier's *Towards an Architecture* (1923), he tries to envision what a house is in its most foundational formulation. "LET US STATE THE PROBLEM. . . . Let us shut our eyes to what exists." What do we glimpse behind our shuttered lids? For Le Corbusier, it is a "shelter against heat, cold, rain, thieves, and the inquisitive. A receptacle for light and sun. A certain number of cells appropriated to cooking, work, and personal life."[1]

There is an unspoken turn in his definition that fascinates me. Within his seemingly neutral description, one cloaked in the fantasy of arch-rationalism that pervades his project as a whole, is a maneuver that undermines the universality it seeks: the collapse of relatively constant existential threats to the human animal ("heat, cold, rain") together with others that are by no means constant—"thieves" and "the inquisitive." These last threats belong to a specific social formation of private property and its

accompanying forms of subjectivity that may have seemed objective or natural to Le Corbusier, but only because he could not perceive the historical particularity of the lived order he existed in, that of capitalism on a global scale.[2] More plainly, there have been and still are (albeit ever fewer) human communities across the globe for whom property, land, and especially living space is not something to be hoarded and defended, but something that constitutively cannot be owned and does not demarcate a private sphere. Moreover, even Le Corbusier's conceptual operation itself is marked by its time, as this process of transhistorically naturalizing threats to property and propriety while tying them explicitly to claims about human nature, essence, and freedom gradually becomes one of the foundational structures of capitalist society and its defense mechanisms.

Faced with its own incoherence, Le Corbusier's attempted universality therefore turns to a language of looming historical disaster and the stern rationality needed to face it: "Men— intelligent, cold and calm—[who] are needed to build the house and to lay out the town."[3] Such a dialectic of crisis and necessity can be seen not only in a vision of the heroic male "planner," but also in the doubling between the house as a protective shell and an armored masculinity familiar from its gathering fascist formation in the very years the architect was developing these ideas. Much as fascism sought to enact a revolutionary counter-revolution against the threat that communist movements posed to social order, Le Corbusier would quite literally articulate the labor of architecture as staving off the specter of social war, designing and constructing houses and cities to nullify discontent and to hold at bay whoever refused the boundaries of property. Such a comparison might seem unfair, at least until we recall not only his explicit fascistic leanings,[4] and perhaps more significantly, the last words of *Towards an Architecture*: "Architecture or Revolution. Revolution can be avoided."[5] And avoided without calling the cops to quell the riot, because in this vision, architecture has already become the police, mutely dictating who is allowed entrance, what can be touched, and what deserves to be shut outside, no matter the heat, the cold, the rain.

*Without Care*

The name for this process—the normalization of the image of the world as hostile, the blurring of distinct categories of threat and the complex of attempts to ward them off through the production of a policed order—is security. *Security* is a word that has become so ubiquitous as to appear natural, open to being cast back across time and situated, for instance, as the grounding reason to build dwellings in the first place. For this reason, it must be defamiliarized, taken to pieces, and placed back into history to challenge what it excuses and enables.

That's a longer project than I am able to carry out here, especially if we are to account for security not only as a general social conception but also in terms of housing specifically: that is, how security comes to structure both a basic notion of being "housed" (as defense against world) and the diffuse operations of social violence routed through the house as conduit and site of debt, domestic violence, exclusion, and patriarchal family values, not to mention as driver of gentrification and forced dislocation. As a gesture, however, it might be useful to place security in tension with another concept—that of safety—to parse out the difference between a basic need for care and an active structure that seeks to maintain a social order in which care is allowed only insofar as it does not threaten that order. If *safety* (derived from the Latin *salvus*, "without injury") designates a state of being protected from possible harm, *security* (from *securus*, "without care") marks a different and historically shifting distance from threat, one that aims to negate the contradictions generating what will subsequently be coded as danger. Yet this meaning of *security* is by no means constant across its history: in early usage, the word was often used pejoratively to describe persons who were overconfident, aimless, or dangerously careless. It underwent a profound shift across the late seventeenth to eighteenth centuries in Europe, transposing itself from that quality in individuals to, first, *security of state* and, second, *security of property*, and hence of civil society. In this way, the application of security doubles back from subjects to the forces that structure their subjection and subjectivation, the requisite condition that articulates a model of bourgeois personhood—to be at once citizen, producer, consumer, and owner—whose purported universality is constituted by its negation *of* that universality through its fundamental exclusion and partitioning of those who will be denied status as citizen (let alone free humans). Researching "those nebulous targets of bourgeois desire: security, order and accumulation,"[6] Mark Neocleous concludes that "the concept of security thus became the ideological guarantee of the egoism of the independent and self-interested pursuit of property within bourgeois society. In doing so, security became the supreme concept of bourgeois society."[7]

If *security* bears in its etymological depths that basic *without*, we should see it as fully negative in a more general and double sense, shot through with retroactive and self-eroding structures of justification. First, as Neocleous stresses, for how it marks a fundamental *insecurity* of the social form—private property and the divide between public and private life, the two spheres violated by Le Corbusier's "thieves" and "the inquisitive"—that it claims to be the natural province of the human animal. Second, for how it insists that only *without* that amalgamation of threats might one achieve a condition in which citizens may "freely" decide and adequately contribute to the continuation of civil society, while ignoring the fact that the conception of the citizen mobilized in such an argument is already enmeshed in, if not produced by, the discourse

of security itself, which marks the regulation of border and threshold, of who is seen as threat and who is seen as having the inalienable right to reside, from a national to neighborhood scale.

In this sense, it is unsurprising how much the language of security continually commingles with, and draws from, immunological frameworks couched in terms of resilience and the fantasy of health under assault by "contagion" and sickness easily assigned to "alien bodies" or polluting matter. On this ground, it easily opens out to fantasies of purgation, social hygiene, and sanitation, operations inseparable not only from explicitly xenophobic and ethnic-nationalist formations but also from the history of policing, especially visible in the ongoing inheritance from early models of law enforcement as dedicated to upholding a general conception of "good order," which might be materially produced by preventing the toxic (that is, politically incendiary) admixture of classes, populations, or races.[8] Moreover, *security* names more than just that familiar form of transposition between the health of the individual body and the health of the "body politic." As Michel Foucault details, it also designates an apparatus of governance that shifts away from the punishment or disciplining of individuals for their violation of Law toward a model that deals with *populations*, and treats such violations as unavoidable, like natural elements of a particular historical order. Yet for the apparatus of security, this inevitability doesn't spell defeat. Instead, it conceives of such social ills as thinkable within "a series of probable events," averages that mark a range from the "optimal [to] a bandwidth of the acceptable that must not be exceeded."[9] In this way, the inevitable is made historical once more, subject to management, calculation, and, above all, neutralization.

These two paths give us a way to grasp the key elements of security. In one regard, a set of concrete mechanisms for the maintenance of "good order" that justifies itself in terms of the logic of individual citizens, whose freedom is possible only in a general condition of national and economic security. In another, a logic of averages, probabilities, allowable losses, and total indifference to any sense that the project of all governance should be to aim, however impossibly, for the security not of *all* (a general population) but of *each and every one*. But following both aspects, we can see how *security* further designates, first, the attempted structuring of processes so as to ward off and buffer all that is seen to destabilize the functional and/or homogeneous assemblage within which they occur, and, second, the presumption that *without* those external threats, such an assemblage would be "healthy" and coherent. In so doing, security allows and fosters the same operation evident in those "primitive" parables of housing, radically flattening and blurring together constitutively different kinds of potential risks into a unified, and necessarily nebulous, array of that which will allegedly ruin our livelihood.

What I am suggesting is not a speculative reading of security's possible meaning. It is, for instance, quite plainly the structure and remit of the Department of Homeland Security, signed into law in 2002 in response to 9/11, to gather beneath the banner of security an absurdly wide array of tasks: critical infrastructure, transportation security, secret service, "emergency management" and disaster response, border protection, weapons of mass destruction mitigation, law enforcement training, cybersecurity, "animal disease" control, long-term policy planning, federal protective service, Coast Guard activities, and last, but not least, citizenship and immigration control, including not only the direct police function of Immigration and Customs Enforcement (ICE) but also the mechanisms of citizenship itself. For such a project of buttressing the crumbling edifice of American hegemony, floods and undocumented migrants are functionally similar: they will make the homeland unlivable if unchecked.

What of the house itself? How does it—as lived space, historical form, fantasy, template, banality, refuge, and nightmare—relate to the broader apparatus of security? One point of departure might be to trace the interchange and eventual obliteration of any clear divide between a sense of public and private security within architectural thinking. Contemporary history makes clear just how much inherited models of fortification, defense, and management cannot be restricted to public buildings or literal borders. The interpenetration of the military and the domestic—developed first in explicitly colonial zones before being reabsorbed into imperial centers—is by now a fundamental element in the conception of housing. It ranges from the erasure of distinct military theaters toward a generalized "threatscape" that wages war from the desktop to the sanitation facility, fields to server farms and back again; the televisual and digital transmission of images of armed conflict as spectacle into the home; and an extension of models of vision initially associated with war (massively extended surveillance, incursion into private spheres) into a permanent condition of emergency. As Beatriz Colomina puts it plainly, the "house is a military weapon, a mechanism within a war where the differences between defense and attack have become blurred."[10]

Yet we might also understand the house as naming arguably the most overdetermined figure and site of security's negotiation between individuals, property, and all that might threaten the bond between the two and dispossess persons of their way of life and accumulated goods, including the house itself. This is especially so given the cost of housing, especially in the Global North. If owned, the house is by and large the most expensive commodity in one's possession, and for this reason, barring the exception of the rich, it can be owned only by borrowing heavily against one's future potential. The house in which one "builds a life" is literally staked on that life continuing to be profitable, making the icon of security into a space saturated with anxiety over its own loss, and the quantity of money involved means that even having one's name on the title is little real guarantee against possible foreclosure or repossession.

What I'm gesturing toward is the latent hostility and uncertainty toward the house that can linger beneath the experience of comfort, stability, and purported safety it provides. This unease

is operative even for the creditworthy, but it is omnipresent for those judged to be "risky ventures" or "subprime," those who are not granted the right to legally remain where they live, those who are expelled from their home-lands, and those who are systematically denied any sense of adequately belonging, above all as a consequence of security's continual racialization of borders and the spaces they frame. Consider, for instance, the double bind for undocumented persons in the United States during and after events such as the 2017 Hurricane Harvey. The images that flowed out from Houston and its surroundings were uncanny, to say the least, a displaced prosaic surrealism unmaking the basic sense of where things belong: the highway is a river, rafts float over chainlink fences, and turbid water enters the house uninvited through a second-story window. Yet the force of such images is not in their depiction of a "universal" disaster that hit all equally. Rather, the turbulent unseating of visual familiarity inadvertently exposes the hostile forces and inversions already gathering at, around, and inside the homes of those never allowed to truly be "home," above all the undocumented populations of the city.

In past years, ICE policy—issued by previous head John Morton—primarily targeted people who were seen as threats to "national security, public safety, and border security." In recent years, it has also dramatically shifted to their houses, with agents going door to door in Latinx neighborhoods to violate the one space thought to be somewhat safe, especially as compared with the dangerous public ground to be covered between work and home.[11] Yet when the flood surged in, many immigrants were afraid not only of the lethal waters entering their homes but also of the evacuation sites designated as refuge points, where ICE would seek to identify and deport them.[12] They were left with nowhere safe to go, both in the present and the future, because after the disaster nominally ended (for the media, at least), the only way undocumented persons could qualify for flood assistance to rebuild the homes where they might be protected from the active predation of "security" forces was if they had a US-born child, thereby furthering the natalist-futurity of the home as first and foremost a "natural" site of reproduction. In short, within a situation that yoked together disparate registers of security, from critical infrastructure failure to natural disasters to citizenship enforcement, those who have been continually defined as a lurking threat to the security of a nation—the functionality of which is significantly enabled by their low-wage work—were made to be *unhomely*. They lived, in other words, the startling inversion and ruination of safety that the apocalyptic images of the flood proffered as exception.

*La casa toma la casa*

My text has, from the start, been haunted and driven by another: Julio Cortázar's 1946 "Casa tomada," which literally names in its title a subject and threat—dispossession—which, I would argue, lies at the center of *security* and *housing's* tangled juncture. The story demands to be read allegorically, especially given the context of contemporaneous political events in Argentina—a sequence of turbulent coups and the onset of Peronism—and its central plot: a pair of bourgeois siblings find their tremendous inherited mansion gradually invaded by unknown forces or assailants, who might be easily coded as surging populism coming to reappropriate the wealth. But if this sort of allegory is made possible by how the story does *not* specify the cause of the events or the identity of the intruders, something peculiar happens in how this uncertainty is written, supplying an *or* (in Spanish, *o*) each time the narrator searches for an answer (such as "I heard something in the library or the dining room"). The result is that we remain caught in the grip of a threat that cannot be identified; it splits between wholly divergent possibilities, yet is processed as absolute violation of property and safety. The story suffuses the house with the nightmare of security turned back on itself, made autonomous, in such a way that the slightest sound can conjure the full array of perceived dangers to civil society: diseases, thieves, floods, immigrants, none or some, one or all. The house is *tomada* politically and metaphysically, expropriated and self-haunted, becoming the site of a ghost story of architectural revolt and a story of the ghosts of past revolt, overdetermined by the weaponized uncertainty of security itself.[13] All we can say, finally, is that the house, as matrix and accumulator of security, has invaded itself. *La casa toma la casa.* Approaching tautology, the notion begins to collapse into itself. So does security, in its relentless self-justification, its terminal indeterminacy, its casting itself back across millennia to claim that it has always been and must always be this way. We build frantically against, only to realize, with horror, that we have been building for.

## ENDNOTES

1. Le Corbusier, *Towards an Architecture*, trans. Frederick Etchells (New York: Dover Publications, 1986), 114.

2. Le Corbusier wasn't alone in this. See Gottfried Semper, for instance: "There is no need to prove in detail that the protection of the hearth against the rigors of the weather as well as against attacks by wild animals and hostile men was the primary reason for setting apart some space from the surrounding world. . . . Enclosures, fences, and walls were needed." Gottfried Semper, quoted in Wolfgang Hermann, *Gottfried Semper: In Search of Architecture* (Cambridge, MA: MIT Press, 1984), 199.

3. Le Corbusier, *Towards an Architecture*, 127.

4. Joseph Nechvatal, "Revisiting Le Corbusier as a Fascist," *Hyperallergic*, July 10, 2015, https://hyperallergic.com/221158/revisiting-le-corbusier-as-a-fascist/.

5. Le Corbusier, *Towards an Architecture*, 289.

6. Mark Neocleous, *War Power, Police Power* (Edinburgh, UK: Edinburgh University Press, 2014), 3.

7. Mark Neocleous, *The Fabrication of Social Order: A Critical Theory of Police Power* (London: Pluto Press, 2000), 43.

8. See, for instance, Patrick E. Carroll, "Medical Police and the History of Public Health," *Medical History* 46, no. 4 (October 2002): 461–94.

9. Michel Foucault, *Security, Territory, Population: Lectures at the Collège de France, 1977–78*, ed. Michel Senellart, trans. Graham Burchell (New York: Palgrave Macmillan, 2007), 6.

10. Beatriz Colomina, "Domesticity at War," *Assemblage*, no. 16 (December 1991): 17.

11. I believe that this alone is what we should mean by "domestic terrorism," against those who use it to shore up the racial matrix of the settler colonial project: the willful conversion of sites of dwelling into sites of absolute fear and anxiety by means of police and governmental bodies.

12. See, for instance, Lorena O'Neil, "An Undocumented Journey through Harvey," *Esquire* online, August 31, 2017, https://www.esquire.com/news-politics/a57277/undocumented-immigrant-hurricane-harvey/.

13. It is interesting to note that the word *tomar* itself carries the autochthonous sense of bearing its own indeterminacy and origin. As Thomas Walsh notes, "Of the forty most frequently occurring verbs in Spanish . . . only one defies easy association to a well known and amply recorded Classical Latin base. Indeed, the sources of the others are so transparent as never to have provoked a hint of scholarly controversy. The resister is *tomar* 'to take,' a form unknown outside the confines of Hispano-Romance." Thomas J. Walsh, "The Etymology of Hispano-Romance *Tomar* 'To Take,'" *Hispanic Review* 68, no. 3 (Summer 2000): 243–65.

# IF THY RIGHT EYE OFFEND THEE

Naomi Beckwith

The monument to Juan de Oñate in Alcalde, New Mexico, can't seem to keep itself together. It's a bronze equestrian statue honoring the "Last Conquistador," a "New World"–born Spanish colonial governor and explorer who, at the tail end of the sixteenth century, claimed vast lands for Spain north of the Rio Grande. Among other things, he founded and planned the present city of Santa Fe, home of SITE Santa Fe's biennial exhibition. Oñate also maintains the dubious distinction of being an exceptionally brutal governor. After a skirmish between one of his captains (his nephew) and the Indigenous Acoma peoples left several men dead, including the nephew, Oñate retaliated with a massacre and mass enslavement of the Acoma. Then, with a touch of medieval cruelty, Oñate ordered the amputation of the right foot of all surviving men above twenty-five years of age. Even the Spanish court was horrified, eventually convicting the governor of unusual cruelty and ordering him to Spain to live out the rest of his days.

The Alcalde monument was erected and dedicated in 1993 by the descendants of Hispanic settlers in the area. In 1997, under cover of night, a group calling itself the Friends of the Acoma cut off the statue's right foot. Simultaneously an act of vandalism and justice, Oñate's dismemberment has found parallels in other parts of the New World. In Martinique's capital, Fort-de-France, a statue of Empress Josephine of France was attacked in 1991. Erected in 1859 to honor the Martinique-born *béké* who became the consort of Napoleon, the statue was mysteriously decapitated, like a French aristocrat guillotined during the Reign of Terror. Though France had abolished slavery in 1794, Josephine is credited with convincing Napoleon to reinstitute the practice in 1802 in order to protect her family's agricultural enterprises in the Caribbean. Martiniquans who have descended from those enslaved people are less enamored of the empress. Unlike the case of the Oñate statue, whose foot has been replaced, efforts to restore Josephine's head have failed, with protesters later adding blood-red paint around her collar, which runs down her chest to the pedestal on which she stands.

These separate monument desecrations are the result of very similar histories and conditions. The installation of each statue responded to the desire to celebrate a long European legacy in the Americas, even to instantiate the historical contributions of lesser-known communities such as Spanish descendants in the United States and French colonials who supported the economic and political fabric of mainland France. In each case, these celebratory urges have come into conflict with aboriginal and enslaved communities whose own historical narratives serve as refutations of the canonizing enterprise. These two protests, in particular, enact an elegant form of removal with poetic performances of historical gestures that make the monuments more instrumental in their amputated form than they ever were in their wholeness. When does absence become effective? What does it mean to have a fruitful lack? And how does dismemberment take on more meaning as an act of protest on behalf of the aggrieved than the erection of any monument, or even counter-monument, ever could? These question, as posed by the SITE curators and the editors of this volume, are queries of representation—how can or does an artist translate the experience of a person or persons whose house has been taken over?

Many of these questions have been framed, mulled over, and debated in the critical realm of postcolonial theory, and answers continue to evade the participants. Since the entry of postcolonial theory into the art world through Homi K. Bhabha's *The Location of Culture* (which relies on Edward Said's groundbreaking *Orientalism*, in which the author argues that the notions of "East" and "West" are historical constructions), it has become a powerful and productive tool for women and artists of color, especially, to expand and interrogate the dogma of Northern and Western European aesthetic judgments.[1] Postcolonialism has allowed cultural producers to develop new terms and languages with which they can shape images (both literary and visual) as part of a reimagining

of a nation or a people during and immediately after colonial occupation. It has been particularly cogent for those who left their homelands for the colonial metropoles of London or Paris, and is the precursor to, in alliance with, or cross-pollinating projects across the globe. Allied movements include *négritude* in the Francophone areas of the Caribbean and Africa, and identity politics in North America.

If these projects have a central protagonist, it is the colonized intellectual who straddles the cultural affect of their natal land and the educational effect of their colonizer. Gayatri Spivak's formative feminist critique of postcolonial studies reminds us that the terms of one's expression are from a borrowed language that can be complicit in reinscribing the very terms one seeks to interrogate; the colonized intellectual's "privilege is their loss."[2] If the necessary operations of the colonial subject are adaptation and synthesis, then some of the questions these strategies raise have gotten thornier in the age of appropriation and cultural ownership. And, for the sake of this project in 2018: How does one conceive and make images a national or cultural project while being, in some cases, a generation or two removed from occupation, and in others, still existing under occupation? The heyday of decolonization occurred in the 1960s, yet that time cannot be the marker of all postcolonial movements. Many nations formed only in the 1990s (Eritrea) or have yet to come into being (Catalunya or Martinique). And many more nations contend with the lingering effects of colonial structures and enterprises on their markets (Nigeria) or on their reputations and ability to participate in international fora (most of the Indigenous peoples of North and South America). Above all, the psychological effects of colonialism remain long after the colonizer packs up and returns to their metropolis. Hence the belated yet impassioned protest resulting in Oñate's missing a foot and Josephine a head.

Though we find symmetry in protests undertaken at very different places and under different political conditions, in relation to the exhibition *Casa tomada* it is useful to examine their divergences. The Oñate protest originated in a group whose house has been taken over. Similarly, Hock E Ayi Vi Edgar Heap of Birds, of the Cheyenne/Arapaho Nation, takes up Spivak's dilemma, explicitly appropriating his occupier's language in order to highlight their national creeds as an ensemble of moral shortcomings. In his print suite *Genocide and Democracy*, Heap of Birds remixes excerpts of revered national texts and lyrics—the US national anthem and the Pledge of Allegiance, for example—with references to Indigenous death and disenfranchisement. Poetic displacement reenacts the historical displacement of Indigenous people to inscribe an ongoing history of violence into the US national mythos.

In the case of the Josephine decapitation, the protesting group had not been taken over in situ but, rather, forcibly relocated to a distant and hostile land. In the prolonged terror of the trans-Atlantic Triangle Trade, buyers and sellers systematically and deliberately stripped their slaves of their native languages and cultures, leaving millions bereft of shared cultural affinities. Indeed, the condition of the African people in the Americas has been one of displacement to a penal condition or, as Huey Copeland would term it, fugitivity.[3] As a fugitive, one is rendered not only homeless, but deprived of the very idea of rootedness, since sitting still results in captivity and destruction. How then to legitimate a form of cultural production that emerges from a condition of instability? For some, the answer was to reconstitute an African homeland, which inspired Pan-Africanism and, in the US, several incarnations of a "Back to Africa" movement.

This could end only in heartbreak. As Saidiya Hartman so eloquently recounts in *Lose Your Mother*, her Ghanaian travels and search for a homeland led her to the realization that "home" exists only as a collective imaginary.[4] She expected kinship in Ghana but, as an African-American woman, felt alienated from those in Africa whose ancestors evaded enslavement. Hartman was not the African she had imagined herself to be, after all, and had to divest herself of the fantasy of a maternal homeland. Yet the loss of Africa as the motherland need not be traumatic, and here it may be useful to return to Spivak, though this time with an inversion: perhaps "loss is their privilege."

Hartman had to acknowledge that she is the product of a distinct, deracinated cultural landscape. Stripped of their African traditions, Black people have replaced those practices with their own. While many see this new culture as lacking an "authentic" relationship to Africa, the achievement of Black fugitives of the Americas is to have produced powerful modes, meanings, sounds, images, and languages in a condition of "freefall," as the artist and filmmaker Arthur Jafa puts it.

Sable Elyse Smith's *Men Who Swallow Themselves in Mirrors*, 2017, captures freefall in a montage video that lacks a clear narrative yet makes instructive use of silence, inversion, and appropriation. Inspired by father's incarceration, Smith creates a meditation on masculinity and the ways in which affection and aggression always coexist in a single consciousness. Indeed, halfway through the video, there is an aerial shot of a cityscape with a body falling in such slow motion that it seems to be in deep-space orbit above the landscape. This scene is a powerful illustration of fugitivity as a state of perpetual motion and precarity.

Smith's work originates from a cultural tradition that holds, perpetually and simultaneously, trauma and ecstasy—never being able to separate the two or to avoid looking back to Africa for validation. Jafa, whose video works also take the form of montage, was once asked in an interview whether his cultural production wasn't about creating a "pastiche" that reflects an absence of both canons and materials. The artist replied:

*It's a pastiche. But at the same time, when you use the word "pastiche," it has a slightly negative connotation, as if it is less authentic. Black being is completely bound up in untenable circumstances. Black people figured out how to make culture in free-fall. We are a nation, but we have no land. There is no Constitution of Black Culture. How do you make culture and community in the absence of all of these things that would simply be a given necessity to create community? It's one of the more fascinating questions of the 20th century and 21st century. Where is the black community going, that big and abstract notion in and of itself?*[5]

What Jafa describes isn't so much a synthesis of the colonizing and native cultures as a novel incarnation by the dispossessed in the "home" of the master. This narrative involves a key intellectual critique: In the recursive and regurgitative moments of speaking, critiquing, and deconstructing language and privilege, we must remember the real and powerful affective relationships. Contemporary art, and perhaps protest gestures, glean their power from mining and giving agency to these feelings of loss and trauma. As we see in the case of the Oñate sculpture in New Mexico and the Josephine statue in Martinique, it may be productive to lose one's parent figure, with, to borrow another phrase from Spivak, "no possibility of nostalgia for that lost Origin."[6]

ENDNOTES

1.  Homi K. Bhabha, ed., *Nation and Narration* (New York: Routledge, 1990); Edward Said, *Orientalism* (New York: Vintage Books, 1979).

2.  Gayatri Spivak, "Can the Subaltern Speak?," in Bill Ashcroft, Gareth Griffiths, and Helen Tiffin, *The Empire Writes Back: Theory and Practice in Post-Colonial Literature* (London: Routledge, 1989), 28.

3.  Huey Copeland, *Bound to Appear: Art, Slavery, and the Site of Blackness in Multicultural America* (Chicago: University of Chicago Press, 2013).

4.  Saidiya Hartman, *Lose Your Mother: A Journey Along the Atlantic Slave Route* (New York: Farrar, Straus, and Giroux, 2007).

5.  In Kate Brown, "'Black People Figured Out How to Make Culture in Freefall': Arthur Jafa on the Creative Power of Melancholy," interview, artnet website, February 21, 2018, https://news.artnet.com/art-world/arthur-jafa-julia-stoschek-collection-1227422.

6.  Spivak, "Can the Subaltern Speak?," 28.


FOLLOWING SPREAD: Victoria Mamnguqsualuk, *Flesh Eating Monster,* 1984

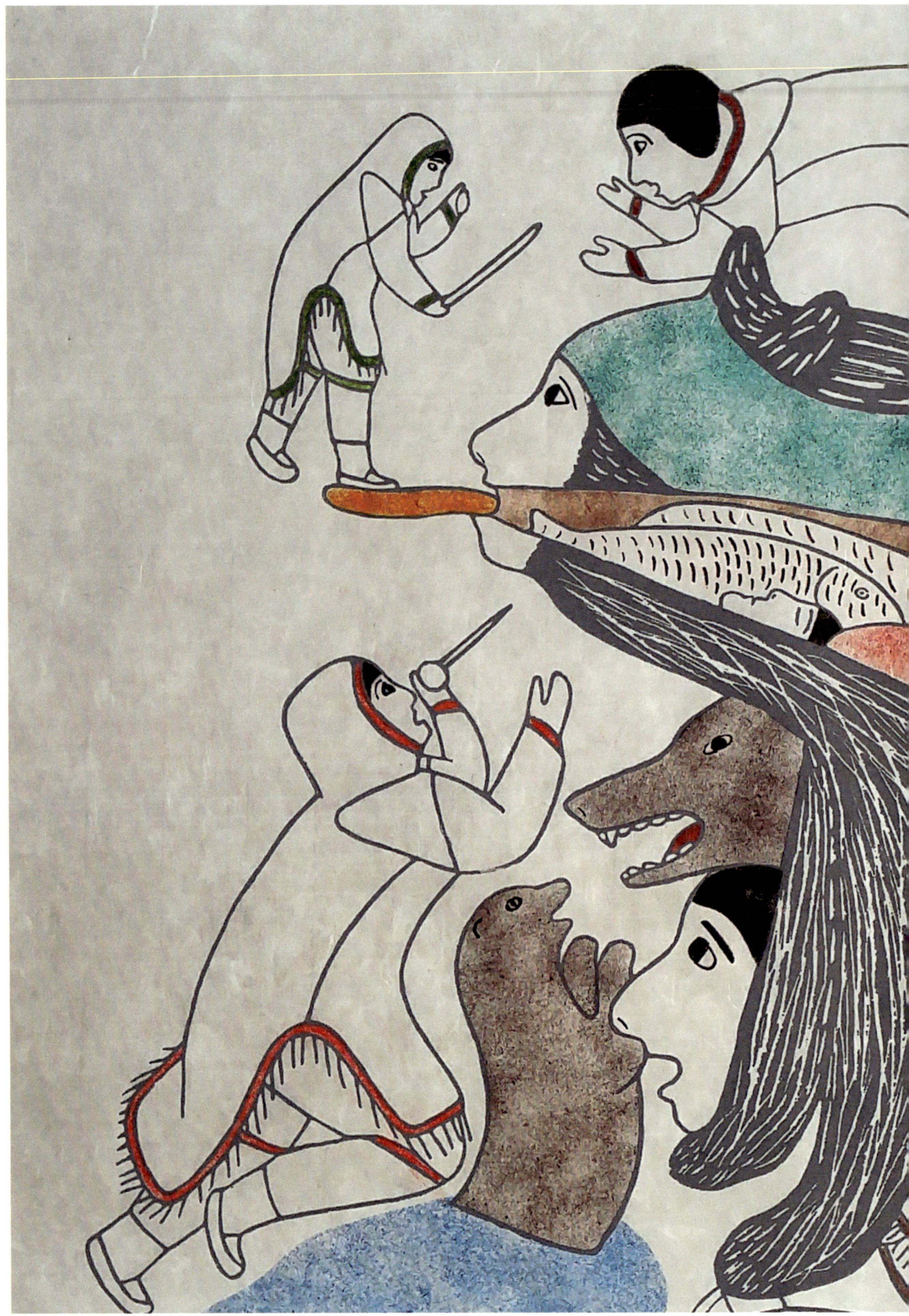

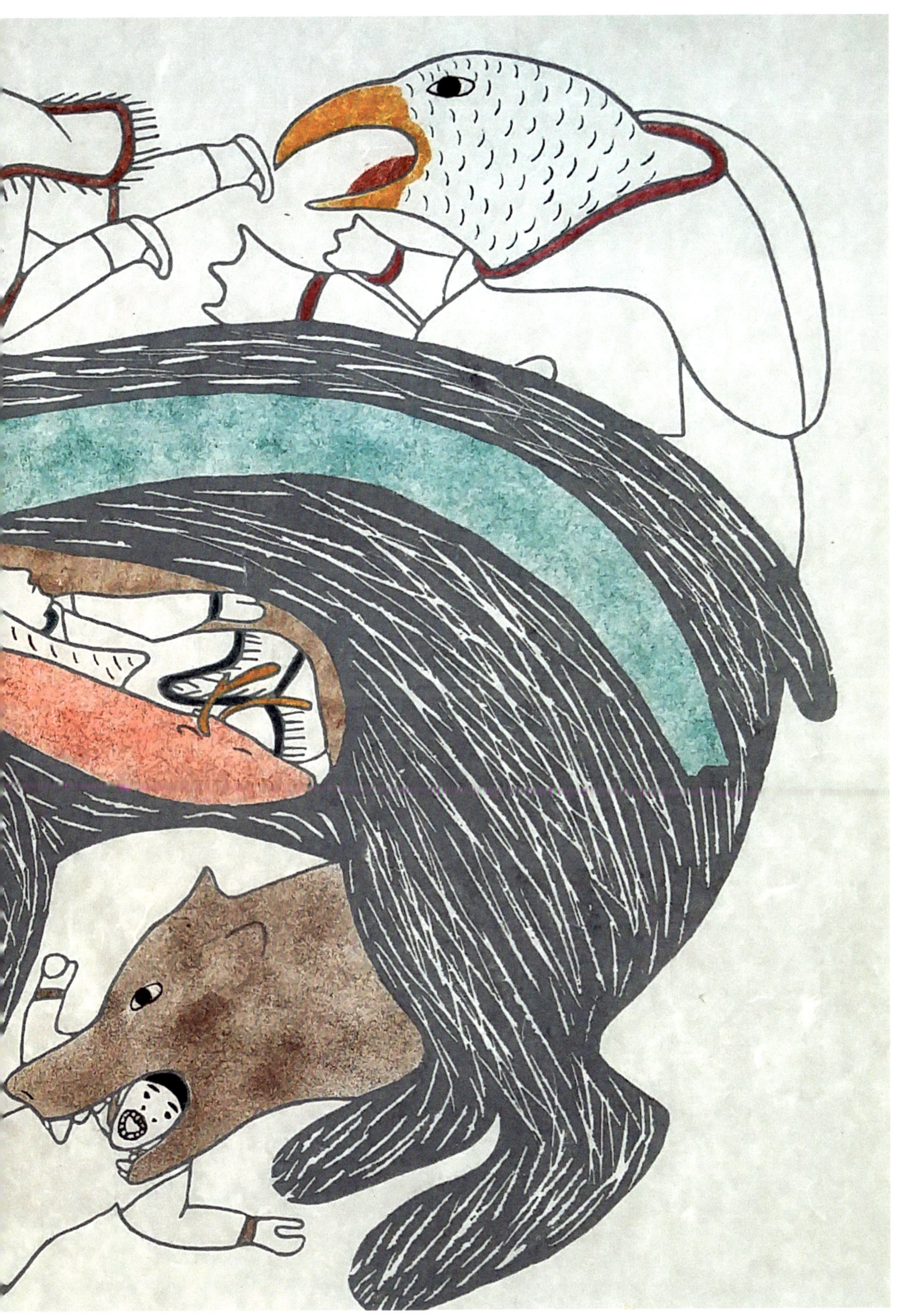

# ACKNOWLEDGMENTS

Realizing this ambitious exhibition would not have been possible without the commitment and hard work of many colleagues and collaborators. I am grateful to all who supported and dedicated themselves to this important project.

My appreciation goes first to the extraordinary team of thinkers who conceived and brought together the exhibition: co-curators José Luis Blondet, Candice Hopkins, and Ruba Katrib, and curatorial advisor Naomi Beckwith.

The curatorial team was supported by an equally stellar and tireless team at SITE Santa Fe. Working closely with the curators was Brandee Caoba, Assistant Curator, who lent her attention to every aspect of the project, including its many new commissions. We owe huge thanks as well to Sage Sommer, Exhibitions Manager and Registrar, who coordinated the complex installation, kept a steady eye on planning, and managed the complex details of bringing the artworks safely to SITE. Special thanks go to the installation team who, under the direction of John Cross, our gifted Lead Preparator, skillfully executed the physical implementation of the show.

Many other staff members throughout the SITE building helped in critical ways to make this exhibition a reality. We are grateful to Joanne Lefrak, Director of Education and Curator of Public Practice, for her instrumental work establishing the vision of SITE Center as a hub for *SITElines* programming and long-term community-engaged artist projects, which are expanding and deepening our connection to place and community. Within the Education Department, we also thank Winoka Begay, Indigenous Outreach Coordinator, for her thoughtful input into our discussions on how to present the contentious monument to Spanish conquistador Juan de Oñate sited in northern New Mexico. We thank Anne Wrinkle, Director of External Affairs, for skillfully leading our marketing and public relations efforts and gaining greater visibility for our work. We thank Cathy Putnam, Deputy Director and Chief Financial Officer, for supporting our work every step of the way. We acknowledge the unflagging efforts of SITE's Development Department, including Paisley Mason, Individual Giving Manager; Kate Kita, Grants Manager; Johanna Frenz, Events Manager; Bethany Morse, Events Assistant and Hospitality Coordinator; and Tim Scott, Development Assistant, who have focused their energies on fundraising for the exhibition and planning for the extraordinary events that celebrate it. Special thanks go to Josie Butler, Executive Assistant, for skillfully juggling so much, including but not limited to details concerning our research, communications, and hospitality. We also wish to acknowledge the work of Thomas Patier in New York and Kelly Tsipni-Kolaza in Athens, Greece, who collaborated with our team at SITE and assisted our curators in their offices.

In the community, colleagues and collaborators generously shared their insights into the history of the Oñate monument: Jamison Chas Banks, Adjunct Professor of Printmaking, Institute of American Indian Arts; Rick Hendricks, State Historian; Matthew Martinez; artist Nora Naranjo Morse; Lieutenant Governor Ohkay Owingeh; Patsy Phillips, Director, IAIA Museum of Contemporary Native Arts (MoCNA); Charlene Teters, Dean, Institute of American Indian Arts; and Brian D. Vallo, Director of Indian Arts Research Center, School for Advanced Research. At the Northern Rio Grande National Heritage Area, we thank Thomas Romero, Executive Director; Leland Chapin, Gallery Curator and Social Media Strategist; and Sandy Cata, Office Manager and Grants Coordinator. On behalf of the team I offer special acknowledgment of filmmaker Chris Eyre, who served as intermediary and facilitator in our efforts to represent the 1997 action on the Oñate monument in the exhibition.

The following helped us realize a number of new commissions: Christy Downs, Director, Railyard Park Conservancy; Michael McCabe, Fourth Dimension Fine Art Press; Nikkol Brothers, Visions of Santa Fe; Robert Randazzo, Absolutely Neon, Albuquerque; Santa Fe Railyard Art Project committee members; and Keith Wilkinson, Keith Wilkinson & Company.

Also crucial to the project was the kind assistance of the staff at many galleries and artists' studios, including Ana Castella, José Garcia (joségarcía, mx), Mexico City; Marie Catalano, JTT, New York; Pat Feheley and Elyse Jacobson, Feheley Fine Art, Toronto; Nora Fisch, Galería Nora Fisch, Buenos Aires; Simon Griffiths and Andrew Kirkpatrick, Inuit.Net, Vancouver; William Huffman, Dorset Fine Arts, Toronto; Robert Kardosh and Charles Bateman, Marion Scott Gallery, Vancouver; Sarah Macaulay and Nikki Peck, Macaulay & Co Fine Art, Vancouver; Carolyn Melenani Kuali`i, Kua`aina Associates, Berkeley, CA; Katherine Siboni, Greene Naftali Gallery, New York; Richard Telles and Matthew Lax, Richard Telles Fine Art, Los Angeles; and Rachel Uffner, Rebekah Chozick, and Allison Cooper, Rachel Uffner Gallery, New York.

We are grateful for the generosity of the following private lenders in entrusting us with their works: Adam Gianotti, New York; Samuel La Fountain, Santa Fe; Alain and David Macklovitch, Los Angeles; Franci Neely, Houston; Inna and Michael O'Brian, Vancouver; John and Joyce Price, Mercer Island, Washington; Tracey and Phillip Riese, New York; Joshua Rose, Scottsdale, Arizona; Marnie Schreiber, Burlington, Canada; Carla Shen, New York; Malia Sias, New York; Laura Skoler, New York; and Elena Tavecchia, New York. We also thank the staff of museums, government entities, and foundations who facilitated important loans from their collections: Stephen Borys, Director and CEO, Andrew Kear, Chief Curator and Curator of Canadian Art, and

Nicole Fletcher, Collections Manager, Winnipeg Art Gallery; Errin Copple, Senior Associate Registrar, Los Angeles County Museum of Art; and Krista Zawadski, Curator of Inuit Art, Government of Nunavut Fine Art Collection.

For pulling together works from these and other sources, we wish to credit the important role played by Bob Simon and his stellar logistics team at TCI, Transport Consultants International, Cranford, New Jersey.

For the launch of the show, John Melick, Andy Cushman, and the team at Blue Medium in New York guided our national PR efforts and propelled our work onto a larger stage. We thank them for their outstanding work. We would also like to recognize designers Noah Venezia and Keri Bronk of Venezia-Bronk, who created the show's elegant graphic identity and developed its microsite.

For their unwavering belief in our projects, we are profoundly grateful to SITE Santa Fe's Board of Directors. Under the steadfast leadership of Andrew Wallerstein, the Board contributes immeasurably to our work, engaging enthusiastically with the bold direction of *SITElines*. We are especially grateful for the leadership support committed by SITE Board Members Jeannie and Mickey Klein, John and Anne Marion, Marti Meyerson and Jamie Hooper, Louisa Sarofim, Andrew Wallerstein and Mary Sloan, Jim Manning and Dana Pope Manning, Marleen De Bode Olivié and Marc Olivié, and Carl and Marilynn Thoma.

For championing our show early on with vital and generous support, we wish to acknowledge The Andy Warhol Foundation for the Arts. Additional grants from Avalon Trust, Thornburg Investment Management, and the Villa Aurora and Thomas Mann House e. V. have provided crucial support for the exhibition. The Canada Council for the Arts supported the participation of Canadian artists. Richard Telles funded the transport of Victor Estrada's works. We thank them all.

The richness of this catalogue is in large measure due to our guest writers Magalí Arriola, Naomi Beckwith, and Evan Calder Williams. Their contributions add to the depth of the publication and the dialogue around the exhibition. We are indebted to David Chickey and Montana Currie of Chickey Design for giving our ambitions vision for the book concrete form through their elegant graphic design. We thank Nora Dolan, Publications Manager, for expertly pulling together the many components of this book and looking after every related detail. We are grateful once again to have worked with Lucy Flint, our talented and patient editor, whose expert guidance has produced another *SITElines* catalogue we can be very proud of.

Finally, we express our deepest gratitude to the twenty-three artists in *Casa tomada*, whose incredible works and probing inquiries help us see our world anew.


— Irene Hofmann

FOLLOWING SPREAD: Paz Errázuriz, from the series *Nómadas del mar* (Nomads of the sea), 1996

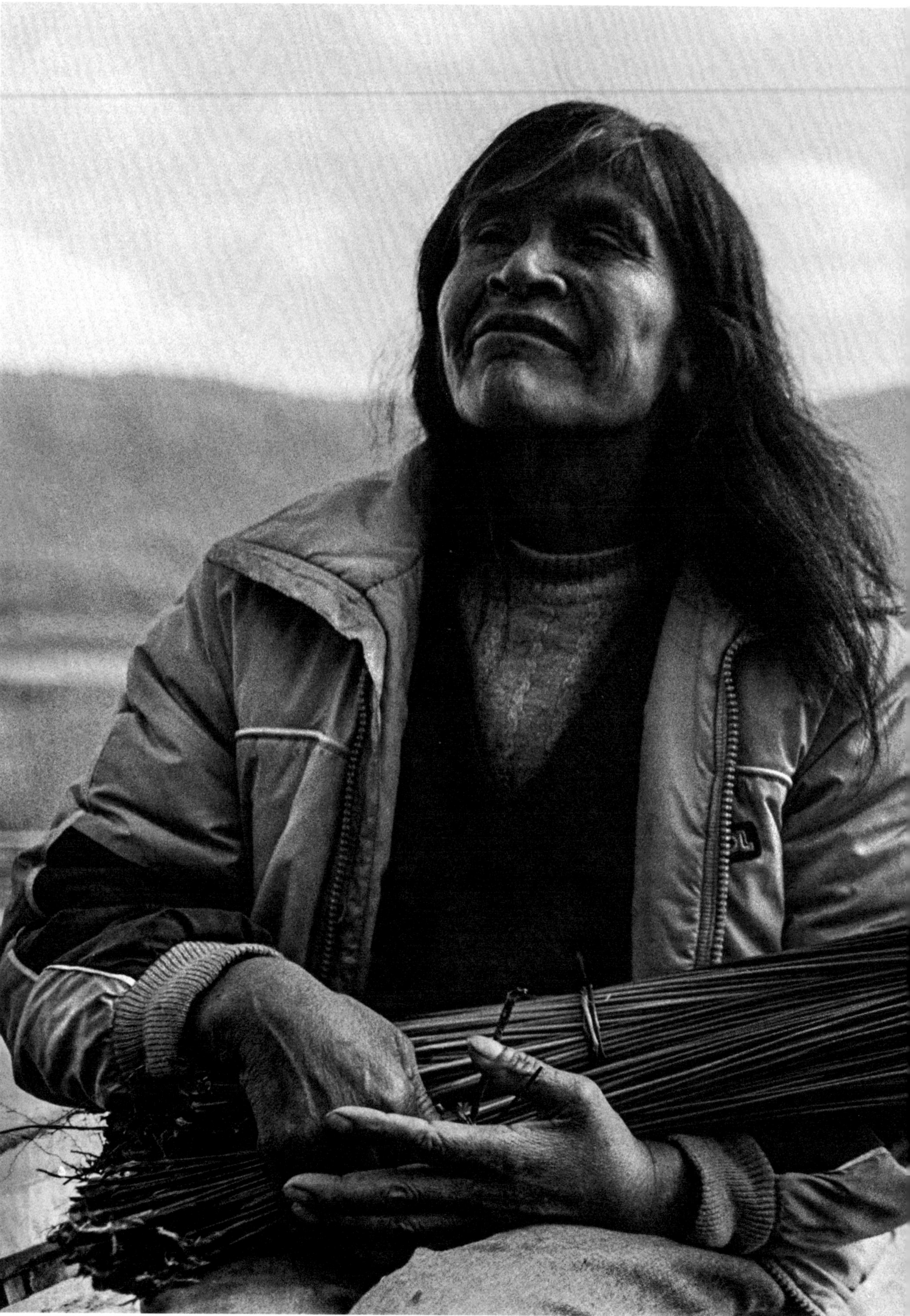

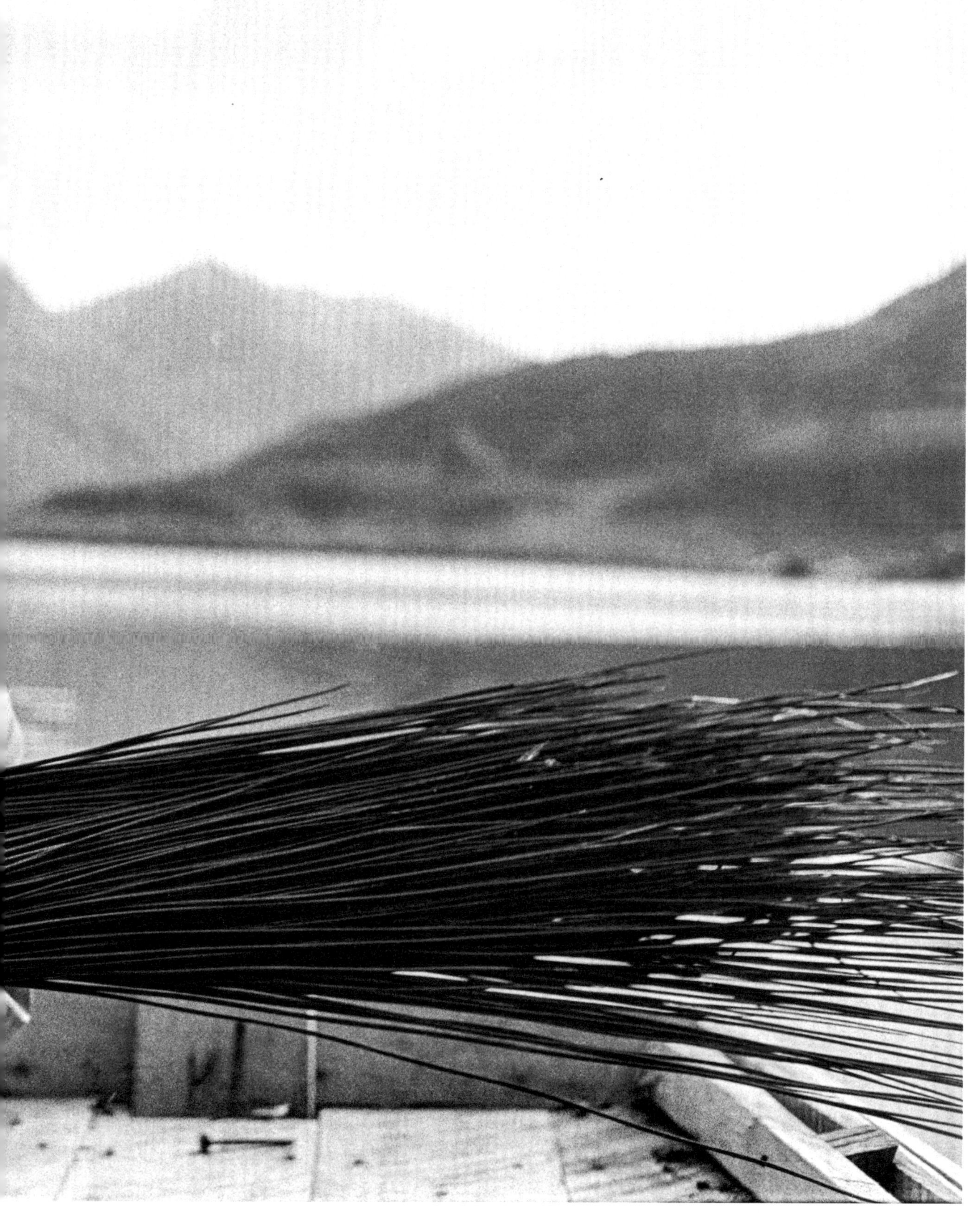

ONE
CANNOT
SPEAK TRUTH
to POWER
If power has
NO USE for
TRUTH.

ON TURN 1 July 201

# CONTRIBUTORS

## Magalí Arriola

(born in Paris, FRA; lives in Mexico City, MEX)

Magalí Arriola is an art critic and independent curator. She is currently KADIST Regional Curator for Latin America. She was Curator at Fundación Jumex Arte Contemporáneo, 2011–14, and Chief Curator at Museo Tamayo, Mexico City, 2009–11. In 2006, she was a visiting curator at the Wattis Institute for Contemporary Art in San Francisco, where she organized *Prophets of Deceit* (2006). From 1998 to 2001 she was Chief Curator at the Museo de Arte Carrillo Gil in Mexico City. Independent projects include *The Sweet Burnt Smell of History: The 8th Panama Biennial* (2008), *What once passed for a future, or The landscapes of the living dead* (Art2102, Los Angeles, 2005), and *Erógena* (Museo de Arte Carrillo Gil, Mexico City / Stedelijk Museum voor Actuele Kunst, Ghent, 2000). Arriola writes books and catalogues and has contributed to periodicals such as *Artforum, Curare, Mousse, Manifesta Journal, The Exhibitionist,* and *Frieze,* where she is Contributing Editor for Latin America.

## Naomi Beckwith

(born in Chicago, USA; lives in Chicago)

Naomi Beckwith is the Marilyn and Larry Fields Curator at the Museum of Contemporary Art Chicago; her exhibitions and writings focus on the impact of identity and multidisciplinary practices in contemporary culture. She previously held positions at the Institute of Contemporary Art in Philadelphia and the Studio Museum in Harlem. Her numerous exhibitions include *Howardena Pindell: What Remains to be Seen* (with Valerie Cassel Oliver) (2018) and *The Freedom Principle: Experiments in Art and Music, 1965 to Now* (with Dieter Roelstraete) (2016–17). She early championed artists such as Lynette Yiadom Boakye, Keren Cytter, Rashid Johnson, The Propeller Group, and Jimmy Robert. In 2015 she served on the jury of the 56th Biennale di Venezia, and received the New Leadership Award from ArtTable, where she is a trustee. A recent fellow with the Center for Curatorial Leadership in New York, Beckwith is a frequent contributor to numerous publications. She holds an MA from the Courtauld Institute in London.

Lutz Bacher, *Whiteboard*, 2018

## José Luis Blondet

(born in Caracas, VEN; lives in Los Angeles, USA)

José Luis Blondet is Curator for Special Initiatives at the Los Angeles County Museum of Art, where he has curated *Liz Glynn: The Myth of Singularity* (2016), *Various Small Fires (Working Documents)* (2015), and *Compass for Surveyors: 19th Century American Landscapes* (2013), and co-curated *A Universal History of Infamy*, part of Pacific Standard Time: LA/LA (2017–18), and *Maria Nordman: FILM-ROOM Smoke, 1967–Present* (2011). He has commissioned performance projects by Liz Glynn, Asher Hartman, La Ribot, Rachel Mason, and Emily Mast, among others. As a guest curator, he has organized two exhibitions with the collections of the CAPC Museum, Bordeaux: *[SIC] Contemporary Nosology* (2017) and *[SIC] Contemporary Nosography* (2016). In 2017, he co-curated *Chalk Circles* at REDCAT, Los Angeles. In 2010, he co-curated *Marta Minujín: MINUCODEs*, at the Americas Society, New York. Blondet previously held positions at the Dia Art Foundation, New York, Boston Center for the Arts, Universidad Central de Venezuela, and Museo de Bellas Artes, Caracas.

## Irene Hofmann

(born in New York, USA; lives in Santa Fe)

Irene Hofmann has been the Phillips Director and Chief Curator of SITE Santa Fe since 2011. She oversaw a $11 million capital campaign to expand SITE's facility with a new building that opened in 2017. Over the last two decades, she has curated or co-curated group exhibitions that include *Future Shock* (2017), *Unsettled Landscapes* (2014), *Agitated Histories* (2011), and *Broadcast* (2009–10), and solo exhibitions by Dawoud Bey, Jason Dodge, Kota Ezawa, Joseph Grigely, Enrique Martinez Celaya, Futurefarmers, Fabrice Gygi, Iñigo Manglano-Ovalle, Marjetica Potr, Mungo Thomson, and others. She is currently working on a large-scale exhibition featuring artistic responses to the global refugee crisis. Hofmann previously held positions at the Contemporary Museum, Baltimore, Orange County Museum of Art, Cranbrook Art Museum, Art Institute of Chicago, Walker Art Center, and New Museum of Contemporary Art. She holds an MA in Modern Art History, Theory, and Criticism from the School of the Art Institute of Chicago.

## Candice Hopkins

(born in Whitehorse, CAN; lives in Albuquerque, USA)

Candice Hopkins is a curator and writer. She was recently named Senior Curator of the Toronto Biennial of Art and is on the curatorial team for the Canadian Pavilion of the upcoming 58th Biennale di Venezia, presenting the work of media art collective Isuma (Igloolik/Montreal). She was a curator for documenta 14 (2017). She was Managing Curator of *SITElines.2016* and co-curator of *SITElines.2014: Unsettled Landscapes* (with Janet Dees, Irene Hofmann, and Lucía Sanromán). Recent essays and presentations include "The Gilded Gaze" for *The documenta 14 Reader*; "The Appropriation Debates" for *Mousse Magazine*; "Outlawed Social Life" for *South as a State of Mind*; and "Native Economies: From the Potlatch Ban to the Masks of Beau Dick," for The Serving Library, Liverpool Biennial. Hopkins has held curatorial positions at the IAIA Museum of Contemporary Native Arts, National Gallery of Canada, and Western Front Society. She is a citizen of Carcross/Tagish First Nation.

## Ruba Katrib

(born in Baltimore, USA; lives in New York)

Ruba Katrib is Curator at MoMA PS1 in New York.
From 2012 to 2018 she was Curator at SculptureCenter,
New York, where she organized the group exhibitions *The
Eccentrics* (2015), *Puddle, pothole, portal* (2014) (with Camille
Henrot), *Better Homes* (2013), and *A Disagreeable Object*
(2012), and solo shows of the work of Kelly Akashi,
Sam Anderson, Teresa Burga, Cercle d'Art des Travailleurs
de Plantation Congolaise, Nicola L., Charlotte Prodger
(all 2017), Rochelle Goldberg, Aki Sasamoto, Cosima
von Bonin (all 2016), Anthea Hamilton, Araya
Rasdjarmrearnsook, Magali Reus, Gabriel Sierra,
Michael E. Smith, Erika Verzutti (all 2015), David
Douard, and Jumana Manna (both 2014). In Chicago,
she co-founded the residency/exhibition space
Threewalls. Katrib has held positions at the Renaissance
Society, Chicago, and the Center for Curatorial Studies
at Bard College, Annandale-on-Hudson. She is an
advisor for the upcoming Carnegie International (2018).
She regularly contributes to museum catalogues and to
periodicals including *Art in America*, *Artforum*, *CURA. Magazine*,
*Kaleidoscope*, *Parkett*, and *Mousse*.

## Evan Calder Williams

(born in Yarmouth, USA; lives in Woodstock)

Evan Calder Williams is a professor at the Center for
Curatorial Studies at Bard College. He is the author of
*Prowling Forms*, *Manual Override: A Theory of Sabotage* (both
forthcoming), *Shard Cinema* (2017), *Combined and Uneven
Apocalypse*, and *Roman Letters* (both 2011). He is the
translator (with David Fernbach) of Mario Mieli's 1977
*Towards a Gay Communism*. His writing has appeared in
*Film Quarterly*, *WdW Review*, *Frieze*, *Cultural Politics*, *La Furia
Umana*, *World Picture*, *The Journal of American Studies*, and
*Estetica*, among other publications. He is an editor of
*Viewpoint Magazine* and a founding member of the film
and research collective Thirteen Black Cats. Williams
was an artist-in-residence at ISSUE Project Room and
has presented solo and collaborative films, performance,
and audio works at venues such as the Biennale de
Montréal, Serpentine Gallery, Mercer Union, Images
Festival, mumok, Festival du Nouveau Cinéma, Whitney
Museum of American Art, and Swiss Institute.

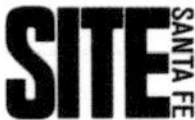

SITE Santa Fe nurtures innovation, discovery, and inspiration through the art of today.

SITE Santa Fe
1606 Paseo de Peralta, Santa Fe, NM 87501 USA  t: 505.989.1199   sitesantafe.org

Available through
D.A.P. / Distributed Art Publishers
155 Sixth Avenue, 2nd Floor, New York, NY 10013 USA  t: 212. 627.1999   artbook.com

ISBN: 978-0-9856602-7-7
Library of Congress Cataloguing-in-Publication Data available from the publisher upon request.

Publications Manager: Nora Kabat Dolan
Editor: Lucy Flint
Design: David Chickey and Montana Currie
Pre-Press: Dexter Premedia Ltd., London, UK


Printed by Editoriale Bortolazzi Stei, Verona, ITA

ázar / Casa Tomada / Ju
ulio Cortázar / Casa Toma
ázar / Casa Tomada / Ju
ulio Cortázar / Casa Toma
ázar / Casa Tomada / Julio
ulio Cortázar / Casa Toma
ázar / Casa Tomada / Julio
ulio Cortázar / Casa Toma